CZECH & SLOVAK
FOOD AND COOKING

CZECH & SLOVAK
FOOD AND COOKING

75 AUTHENTIC RECIPES FROM THE HEART OF EUROPE

IVANA VERUZABOVA

With photography by Martin Brigdale

aquamarine

This edition is published by Aquamarine,
an imprint of Anness Publishing Ltd,
108 Great Russell Street, London WC1B 3NA;
info@anness.com

www.aquamarinebooks.com; www.annesspublishing.com;
twitter: @Anness_Books

If you like the images in this book and would
like to investigate using them for publishing,
promotions or advertising, please visit our website
www.practicalpictures.com for more information.

© Anness Publishing Ltd 2015

A CIP catalogue record for this book is available from
the British Library.

Publisher: Joanna Lorenz
Editorial Director: Helen Sudell
Project Editor: Emma Clegg
Photographer: Martin Brigdale
Home Economist: Katie Giovanni
Stylist: Martin Brigdale
Designer: Lisa Tai
Production Controller: Ben Worley

COOK'S NOTES

- Bracketed terms are intended for American readers.
- For all recipes, quantities are given in both metric and imperial measures and, where appropriate, in standard cups and spoons. Follow one set of measures, but not a mixture, because they are not interchangeable.
- Standard spoon and cup measures are level. 1 tsp = 5ml, 1 tbsp = 15ml, 1 cup = 250ml/8fl oz.
- Australian standard tablespoons are 20ml. Australian readers should use 3 tsp in place of 1 tbsp for measuring small quantities.
- American pints are 16fl oz/2 cups. American readers should use 20fl oz/2.5 cups in place of 1 pint when measuring liquids.
- Electric oven temperatures in this book are for conventional ovens. When using a fan oven, the temperature will probably need to be reduced by about 10–20°C/20–40°F. Since ovens vary, you should check with your manufacturer's instruction book for guidance.
- The nutritional analysis given for each recipe is calculated per portion (i.e. serving or item), unless otherwise stated. If the recipe gives a range, such as Serves 4–6, then the nutritional analysis will be for the smaller portion size, i.e. 6 servings. The analysis does not include optional ingredients, such as salt added to taste.
- Medium (US large) eggs are used unless otherwise stated.
- Front cover shows Roast Goose with Red Cabbage and Lokse – for recipe, see pages 64–65.

PUBLISHER'S NOTE

Although the advice and information in this book are believed to be accurate and true at the time of going to press, neither the authors nor the publisher can accept any legal responsibility or liability for any errors or omissions that may have been made nor for any inaccuracies nor for any loss, harm or injury that comes about from following instructions or advice in this book.

Contents

Introduction   6

History   8

Geography & landscape   10

Food culture & culinary customs   12

Beer & winemaking   14

Festivals & traditions   16

Classic ingredients   18

Soups   **22**

Snacks, appetizers & light meals **36**

Fish, meat & game   **52**

**Sweet mains &
vegetarian dishes**   **88**

Desserts & baking   **108**

Useful addresses   126

Index   127

Acknowledgements   128

Introduction

The Czech Republic and Slovakia nestle together at the heart of Europe, encircled by Germany, Poland, Ukraine, Hungary and Austria. With much history in common, and united as Czechoslovakia from 1918 until 1993, the two countries have a similar culture, language and cuisine, although they have also shared a sometimes turbulent history. Both countries boast breathtaking mountainous landscapes and distinctive architecture that attract tourists from all over the world. The traditional cuisines provide hearty, wholesome meals, and these are heavily influenced by their close European neighbours, Germany, Austria and Hungary.

Alliance and division

There have been many complex changes of power within the Czech and Slovak territories during their history. For a large part of the 20th century the two countries were unified, but in the latter part of the century they split into the

LEFT Czech bride from Kloboučky, Brno, in Moravian national costume.

BELOW LEFT Young man of the 19th century in Slovakian national costume.

BELOW A statue in Bratislava of Milan Rastislav Štefánik, a Slovak who helped achieve Czechoslovak sovereignty, the symbol of which is the lion (below).

Czech Republic and Slovakia. This was a mutual decision based on cultural differences, including conflicting ideas about appropriate political divisions, whether based on sovereignty, confederation or independence. However, the close proximity, a shared history and similar cultural influences give each population much common ground. The countries' relationship is friendly and they enjoy healthy competition in many modern-day sports, including football and ice hockey.

Since the separation of the Czech Republic and Slovakia in 1993 both countries have espoused democratic liberal economic systems. Each economy relies on industrial production,

with a particular presence in automotive and electrical goods. However, the simple peasant folklore and farming traditions that have always structured their working lives still run strongly throughout each culture. This also colours the population's diligent, honest and hardworking approach to life.

Using the book

Introducing a range of authentic dishes, the aim of this book is to give a balanced representation of the traditional cuisines. The intention is also to explain the cookery methods in an accessible way.

Each cuisine does have its own unique identity and culture. Wherever relevant, the recipes attribute the locality of the recipe to the Czech Republic or Slovakia and, in examples where recipes have much in common, will make any possible distinctions clear in terms of ingredients, preparation and tastes. Certainly many dishes have such a long history in the geographical region that it is sometimes hard to attribute them with a clear origin.

The recipes are presented within five chapters. The first, on Soups, is full of regional dishes that are simple, hearty and nutritious. Soups are one of the most deep-rooted culinary traditions in the region – you won't find many Czechs or Slovaks who choose to start their meal without one. The two next chapters

LEFT Young ice-hockey players from Finland and the Czech Republic shake hands after a tournament.

are on Snacks, Appetizers and Light Meals, and Fish, Meat and Game. Here you will find a balance of typical Czech and Slovak dishes, and a large portion of recipes that are shared in both of the cuisines.

Neither the Czech Republic or Slovakia are known for their vegetarian culture. However, there are plenty of recipes to suit a vegetarian lifestyle, and many more that can be adapted to do so. One of the best ways of finding recipes is connected to the longstanding tradition of having a meat-free day every week, typically involving a thick vegetable soup as a starter and a sweet main course to follow. I remember my grandmother offering a tasty vegetable soup and 'buchty' (baked sweet jam buns) as a main course on such days. So the next chapter, called Sweet Mains and Vegetarian Dishes combines these two approaches.

The final chapter, Desserts and Baking, has an emphasis on baked products, because desserts have never been a big feature at mealtimes, with the exception perhaps of simple dishes such as a fruit compôte. Despite this, desserts have become more popular, but the food served before and during the main meal often means there is little room left for a sweet finale, particularly if the main meal consists of a sweet dish.

There are many cakes in this chapter, often served as a tea-time sweet, and also breads. The latter, such as rye bread, play a vital role throughout the book, sometimes as an accompaniment and sometimes as the main ingredient. Baked goods, such as the soft rolls rohlíky (Czech) or rožky (Slovak) are bought daily in the shops, but because they are not easily available outside the two countries, they are included here for authenticity, even though these recipes can be more time-consuming to prepare.

Some of the common ingredients in the recipes, such as povidla or slivkový lekvar (a thick plum jam), the specialist types of flour, and tvaroh (a type of soft cheese), are local and can be hard to source outside of the country of origin. In these cases, listed alternatives are included that work just as well, such as substituting Quark cheese for tvaroh cheese, or Brie or Camembert for Hermelín cheese.

BELOW A farmer with two bulls drawing a cart in the Czech Republic.

History

The central location of the Czech Republic and Slovakia have made them targets for occupants and settlers, and for invaders wanting to rule the region. Slav tribes in the region can be traced right back to the countries' early history, and others who have taken or shared control since include Moravians, Bohemians, Germans, Hungarians, Hussites, Habsburgs and Austrians. Both countries have a history of strict religious beliefs but whereas the Slovakian population still has strong Roman Catholic roots, the Czechs have a large number of atheists or agnostics. The Czechs have also absorbed more Western influences than their neighbours.

The Slav tribes

One of the first occupants of the territories that today make up the Czech and Slovak Republics were the Slav tribes in the fifth century AD, who established new homelands after the break-up of the old Roman Empire. They had strong, self-sufficient communities, efficient farming methods, and disruptive military and raiding tactics that kept other tribes at bay.

The Great Moravian Empire

From 830 to 906 AD, what is now the Czech Republic, Slovakia, parts of Germany, Poland and Hungary formed the Great Moravian Empire, encompassing Bohemia, Slovakia, southern Poland and western Hungary. During this time Cyril and Methodius, now celebrated saints, spread their Christian beliefs and roots, as well as the Cyrillic alphabet, which was translated into Slavic.

The Přemysl Dynasty

In the western two-thirds of the Czech Republic lies Bohemia, and the Přemysl Dynasty held power there from the 9th century. The Good King Wenceslas Christmas carol tells of Wenceslas I (907–935), Duke of Bohemia during the early years of this dynasty. The Přemysl rule lasted until 1306, when German King Otto I conquered the Bohemian lands for the Holy Roman Empire, later expanded to Austria and Slovenia. The territories prospered, with Prague a centre of power that flourished economically, shown by the building of its fine Gothic architecture.

Hungarians, Hussites and Habsburgs

In Slovakia, Hungarians conquered the Great Moravian Empire in around 896, and ruled until the collapse of the Austro-Hungarian Empire in 1918. This rule was challenged by the Hussites in the late 14th and early 15th centuries, threatening the established Catholicism, but the Hussites reached a peaceful

LEFT Saint Cyril and Saint Methodius, who brought orthodoxy to the Slavic peoples of central Europe in the 9th century AD.

ABOVE Emperor Sigismund, the King of Hungary and Bohemia (1368–1437).

agreement in 1436 with King Sigismund, of Hungary and Bohemia, also Holy Roman Emperor.

There were struggles for Bohemia throughout the centuries, and in the 13th century and later in the 16th century the German Habsburgs gained some control. The 16th-century occupation turned into the Thirty Years' War (1618–1648) between the strict Habsburg Catholics and the liberal-minded Protestant Bohemians. The Czech defeat by the Habsburgs was followed by Catholicization and Germanization.

During 16th-century Habsburg rule, Hungary had been defeated by the Ottomans and was on the retreat. The Austrian Habsburgs who occupied the Czech lands had taken the Hungarian crown and moved the capital to Bratislava. The Habsburgs defeated the Ottomans and drove them out of Europe.

The end of the 18th century saw the Czech population struggling against Habsburg rule and Slovakia against Hungarian domination. Revolutions were spreading across Europe. In 1867, Austria and Hungary entered into a dual monarchy, the Austro-Hungarian Empire. Slovakia was subjected to a strict programme of Hungarization, with Hungarian taught in schools and the removal of Slovak lands for Hungarians.

Fighting for independence
During WWI the two countries opened a case for their independence with the support of US President Woodrow Wilson. This culminated in the single federal state of Czechoslovakia on 28 October 1918, made up of the two equal Republics. In 1938, Germans in the Czech Sudetenland were suffering discrimination by the Czech population. The Munich agreement in 1938 saw Germany, France, Britain and Italy allow Hitler to annexe this part of the country. In 1939, Germany moved into Bohemia and Moravia and declared these regions their protectorate. For the duration of WWII, Slovakia became an independent state.

Communism
In August 1944, the Slovak National Uprising (SNP) challenged their leader, Jozef Tiso, who was directing the country in a Nazi regime. The uprising was quashed by German troops after two months. After the war, the Communists were voted in, and, in 1948 they took control of the government.

In the Communist era, Slovak interests were overlooked, many people from both countries were imprisoned, executed or died in labour camps, often for non-Communist beliefs.

During the 1960s, the general secretary Alexander Dubček proposed and campaigned for "socialism with a human face". This resulted in Soviet tanks rolling in on the night of 20 August 1968 to restore control.

During the Cold War, the Eastern Bloc was deprived of development. Things remained stable under Communism, but people never gave up. On 17 November 1989, the Communist

ABOVE LEFT Tomas Garrigue Masaryk, Czechoslovakia's first President, entering Prague in 1918.

ABOVE Crowd in Prague celebrating the Velvet Revolution in 1989.

Youth Movement of Prague organized a demonstration that spurred on others in the following days, culminating in 750,000 people dangling their keys in a peaceful protest to tell the Communists to leave their keys on the doorstep. As a result, a new government with a Communist minority was formed. This became known as the Velvet Revolution, because of the calm nature of the demonstrations.

The age of democracy
On January 1993, Czechoslovakia split into the Czech Republic and Slovakia. Both are now parliamentary democracies. Slovakia's road to recovery was not as smooth as the Czech's, halted by the election of Vladimír Mečiar's party into a coalition government in 1994, who opposed any open criticism of the government. These antidemocratic laws brought Meciar's rule to an end in 1998. The Czech Republic joined NATO in 1999, Slovakia joined in 2004, and both countries entered the EU in 2004.

Geography & landscape

The Czech Republic and Slovakia are blessed with spectacular natural landscapes. These include dramatic vistas and exhilarating mountains, alpine scapes, lowlands, forests and rivers. The vast stretches of mountains extend from the Carpathian Mountains in the north of Slovakia to the stunningly beautiful mountains of the Bohemian Forest in the Sumava region of the Czech Republic. The landscape dictates the local land use and agriculture, with the growth of crops such as barley, sunflowers and potatoes along with sugar beet, grapes and hops, the last two giving the raw materials for the burgeoning local production of wine and beer.

Empire, which dates from 962 AD, and of the former Czechoslovakia (1918–1993). The city lies on the Vltava (Moldau) river in central Bohemia. It is full of stunning architecture, including Gothic, Renaissance and Baroque buildings, bridges, churches, castles (Prague castle is the largest in the world), palaces, gardens and a medieval old town. There are also numerous museums and theatres, and a very rich music scene.

LEFT An evening view of St Wenceslas Statue in Prague, the Czech Republic.

The Czech landscape

There are many mountain ranges in the Czech Republic including the centrally positioned Bohemian Massif that encircles a raised basin called the Bohemian Plateau, the Krkonoše Mountains in the north with the highest peak Mount Sněžka, the Hrubý Jeseník Mountains in Moravia and Silesia, the Beskydy Mountains in the eastern Czech Republic and northwest of Slovakia, and the Šumava range along

BELOW Skalnaté pleso is a lake in the Skalnatá Valley in the High Tatras, Slovakia.

The Czech Republic

With Germany to the west, Poland to the north, Slovakia to the east and Austria to the south, the Czech Republic is a landlocked country, with low mountain ranges to the west in Bohemia. The country has 14 regions, each with their own customs, traditions, dialects and folklore. The historic regions of Bohemia, Moravia and Silesia (also called The Czech Lands) provide the most ancient roots of the country's customs and cuisines. Historically these regions were considered as separate countries, and have been controlled by different tribes, emperors, kings and countries through the ages.

The Czech capital, Prague, was also the capital city of the Holy Roman

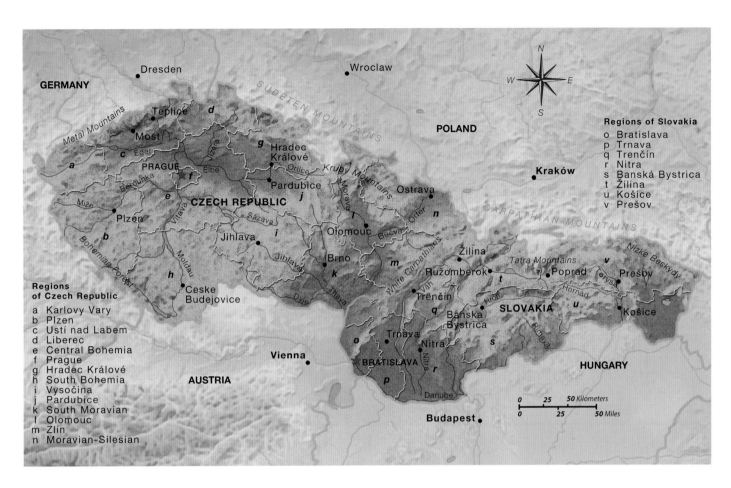

Regions of Slovakia
o Bratislava
p Trnava
q Trenčín
r Nitra
s Banská Bystrica
t Žilina
u Košice
v Prešov

**Regions
of Czech Republic**
a Karlovy Vary
b Plzen
c Ustí nad Labem
d Liberec
e Central Bohemia
f Prague
g Hradec Králové
h South Bohemia
i Vysočina
j Pardubice
k South Moravian
l Olomouc
m Zlín
n Moravian-Silesian

the southern Czech border. Then there are the meandering river valleys and fertile lowlands of South Moravia and the Silesian Lowlands in the north. The main rivers, the Vltava, Morava, Svratka, Svitava, Sázava and Labe, reach their outlets in the North Sea, the Baltic Sea and the Black Sea.

The Slovak Republic

Slovakia shares its border with the Czech Republic, Poland, Ukraine, Hungary and Austria. The country has eight regions, each defined by the area surrounding a city.

Slovakia's capital is Bratislava, which lies on the River Danube and at the foot of the low Carpathians in the south west. The city is situated near the border to Hungary and to Austria and is also close to the Czech border. Because of this, it is animated by contrasting cultural influences and is a popular tourist destination. The city is picturesque, with narrow, winding cobblestone paths,

medieval architecture, historic buildings, museums and Bratislava Castle, a dramatic landmark within the cityscape.

The Slovakian landscape

Distinctive for its mountain ranges, the Slovak landscape includes the Carpathians across the north, part of which is the Tatra Mountains, an alpine landscape and popular skiing resort that forms a natural border between Slovakia and Poland. Slovakia boasts some of the most impressive natural heritage sites and many popular skiing, hiking, cycling, rock climbing and camping tourist destinations. The country is one of the few in central Europe to have brown bears in the High Tatras, the highest mountains in the Carpathian range. The area the bears inhabit has been protected as a National Park, which is managing to preserve their population.

The country is rich in rivers and lakes that rise at the foot of the mountain peaks, explaining the country's

ABOVE The two countries have no natural coastline and a mountainous terrain.

abundance of mineral-water and hot water springs. Slovakia's longest river is the river Vah, flowing from the north to the south where it meets with the Danube.

Agriculture and crops

The landscape of both countries has an established agricultural tradition, mainly of arable crops such as barley, hops, maize, corn, rye and wheat, and a strong association with brewing. In fact, the Czech population has the highest consumption of beer in the world! Other crops include oilseeds, sugar beets and potatoes. Permanent crops include citrus, coffee and rubber, fruit trees, nut trees and vineyards. Pigs, cattle and poultry are the most farmed livestock, although agricultural production, especially of livestock, is in decline, with small farms struggling with a lack of modern technology.

Food culture & culinary customs

The diets of the Czech Republic and Slovakia have been largely shaped by its many invaders and settlers. The diet would traditionally have been starchy and carbohydrate-rich – in previous centuries this would have given the population the strength for the demanding physical work in the fields that was required to survive. Nowadays, in response to changing lifestyles, with less active and demanding everyday work routines, many concessions have been made towards a current-day emphasis on healthy, low-fat cooking. Both cuisines have also readily absorbed food influences from all around the world.

Culinary influences

Slovakia spent time under Hungarian rule, and so this is the most prominent foreign influence on its cuisine. The Czech Republic was for a long period under Austrian and German rule, and this explains the preference for sauerkraut, potatoes, dumplings and meat. Nonetheless, the food traditions of the Czech Republic and Slovakia have characteristic core staples and dishes.

A day's food

Breakfast in both countries consists of a slice of bread or a roll with a savoury or sweet topping, often butter, cheese and ham, or homemade jam or honey, accompanied by black tea with lemon and honey, or coffee.

Lunch is a hearty and filling meal. Invariably starting with a soup, the main course will consist of pork or beef, with a sauce and dumplings. Desserts are rare, especially as the lunchtime meal is so heavy. The ideal accompaniment to this meal is a pint of draught pivo (beer).

Evening dinner is a light meal, often something sweet such as pasta with poppy seeds, accompanied by a hot drink such as tea or cocoa, or a glass of kefir or sour milk. Sometimes it might be simply a slice of bread, similar to breakfast.

Food preparation and family sit-down meals play an important role, although nowadays this is usually reserved for weekends when families make the time to cook elaborate meals together.

Hospitality and entertaining

Both countries are well known for their hospitality. Families and friends will often visit each other from different parts of the country, and there is always a big feast and celebration on such occasions. Both affluent and poor families make their guests as comfortable as possible, and get-togethers are happy ones, with singing, dancing, drinking and feasting. When visitors arrive, the host family typically greets them with a selection of prepared delicacies from the region, accompanied by the local fiery plum brandy (slivovice or slivovica) or home-produced wine.

BELOW LEFT An outdoor restaurant in the old town quarter of Trenčín, Slovakia.

BELOW CENTRE A mountain chalet on the Chopok Peak in the Low Tatras, Slovakia.

BELOW Musicians playing at the famous U Fleků beer cellar in Prague.

Dumplings

Both countries have a long-standing tradition of dumplings. There is a type of light, soft and fluffy dumpling (knedlik in Czech or knedla in Slovak) made from flour, eggs, yeast, and milk, and sometimes baguette cubes. These are made into a long oval and sliced with a cutting thread. They are perfect for soaking up tasty meat sauces. A single portion might be four to eight dumplings, depending on the person's appetite!

Knedlik or knedla are the classic dumplings, but there are other types, which might be served as a side dish or as the main element of a meal, such as halušky. Potato dumplings are popular, less time-consuming to make, and taste wonderful with sauerkraut, spinach, or as an alternative to boiled potatoes (see page 51). These are smaller in shape, but heavier than the classic fluffy flour dumplings (see below).

Dumplings are often served as a light dinnertime meal, by cutting them into cubes, mixing them with an egg or two and frying in a little oil until golden.

ABOVE Koláče are round, sweet buns with poppyseed, curd or jam.

The contemporary kitchen

Many households, especially in rural areas, have a pantry and cellar full of supplies. It is common for people still to make their own jams and marmalades, pickle vegetables such as gherkins and peppers, and stock up on shopping provisions such as canned fruit and vegetables.

During the Communist era, local shops were limited in their stocks, especially of fresh produce, and every day it was quite normal to see long queues in the fruit and vegetable sections. This was harder in the cities because people had no produce from the land to fall back on. In the country, farmers developed great efficiency in storing food and living off the land. In Slovakia, farmers relied on staple ingredients such as potatoes, wheat and cheese, the latter because of the significant sheep farming industry. This emphasis is still evident in the Slovak cuisine, where recipes often contain the same few ingredients cooked in many different ways. Most of these recipes have remained favourites and have stood the test of time.

There is much more room to experiment in the kitchen these days, with easily available fresh and exotic produce. Also, new ingredients are being used in traditional recipes, often to make them healthier or lighter, or to add a new twist to an old classic.

Bread Dumplings (knedlík or knedla)

These dumplings are served with most sauces, sauerkraut dishes and stews. When making them, ensure the yeast is activated and the dough nice and fluffy.

Makes 3 dumplings and 6–8 portions

250ml/8fl oz/1 cup milk, tepid
5ml/1 tsp caster (superfine) sugar
30g/1¼oz fresh yeast
1 egg
2 one-day old rohlíky, or white
   rolls, cut into pieces (see page 124)
400g/14oz hrubá flour, or
   250g/9oz/1½ cups semolina and
   150g/5oz/1¼ cups plain
   (all-purpose) flour, plus extra
     for dusting
5ml/1 tsp salt
3 litres/5¼ pints/12 cups water
a pinch of salt
oil, for greasing

1 In a cup, mix 100ml/3½fl oz/⅔ cup tepid milk with the sugar, and crumble in the yeast. Mix well, cover with a dish towel and leave to stand in a warm place for 10 minutes to become frothy and rise to the top of the cup.
2 Mix the remaining milk with the egg and add the chopped rolls. Soak until the bread has absorbed the liquid.
3 Add the flour, salt and yeast mixture, and mix with a wooden spoon or an electric mixer with bread hook attachment for 5 minutes. Cover with a dish towel, put in a warm place and leave to rise for 2 hours, or until doubled.
4 Knead the dough for 3 minutes. Divide into three equal parts and mould each

into a long oval. Cover with a dish towel and leave to rise for 15 minutes.
5 Bring a large pan of water to the boil, add salt and boil each dumpling for 7 minutes on each side. Remove, pierce each dumpling all over with a fork and brush each one with oil. Use a long piece of thread to cut the dumpling into 2cm/¾in slices to serve.

PER SERVING: Energy 246 kcal/1042kj; Protein 9g; Carbohydrate 49g, of which sugars 3g; Fat 3g, of which saturates 1g; Cholesterol 33mg; Calcium 101mg; Fibre 1g; Sodium 354mg.

Beer & winemaking

Drinking alcohol is an essential part of the culture of both the Czech Republic and Slovakia, and it is usual for alcohol to be on offer at most social gatherings. Because the home brewing of spirits such as Slivovica (plum brandy) or Borovička, a type of gin, is so common, the percentage of alcohol is often high, so beware if you are offered any when visiting. There are many wine and beer festivals that happen in the region throughout the year, including Vinobranie in Pezinok, Slovakia (near Bratislava), a festival celebrating the autumn wine harvest, and the Czech Beer Festival in Prague.

Beer

The historic region of Bohemia has the most beer breweries in the Czech Republic, many recognized in the international market. Czech beer is considered one of the finest in the world, renowned for its clear and refreshing taste. It is also famously produced without any chemicals, which is the reason why it's so easy to drink.

Beer production dates back to the 12th century, and the most prominent cities are Plzeň, the city where pilsner, a type of pale lager, was invented (the city produces Pilsner Urquell). The other most commonly known brands are from České Budějovice, producing Budweiser Budvar, and Prague, producing Staropramen. It is not uncommon for beer to be consumed during the workday and at lunchtime the pubs are always full of thirsty regulars. The Czech term for beer is 'pivo' (pih-voh), and is one of the first words to be learnt by visitors.

Slovakia produces a small number of internationally recognized beers, such as Zlatý Bažant (Golden Pheasant), however since the two countries' separation Slovakia has emerged with fewer breweries than its Czech counterpart. Nonetheless, Slovakia's comparatively smaller economy shows that the country is truly a force to be reckoned with in the production of pilsner beer.

The preferred type of beer is a pale lager, but dark beer is also produced, often 'cut' with lager, whereby you mix a half pint of each – this is delicious! The dark beer has a richer and smoother taste and most pubs will offer at least one choice of dark beer. Czech and Slovak beers are traditionally marked with degrees, which refer to the amount of malt extract involved in the brewing process. The degree usually corresponds to a higher percentage of alcohol volume

ABOVE LEFT Malting barley at the Eggenberg Brewery, Český Krumlov, in the Czech Republic.

LEFT Beer drinkers at the Czech Žatec Harvest Festival, a hop and beer festival held in September to celebrate the hop harvest.

– 10 degrees is usually four percent alcohol volume and 12 degrees is around five percent. The higher degrees give the beer a fuller flavour.

Wine

The production of wine is an integral part of the Czech culture and heritage, especially in the warmer, sheltered parts of Moravia. This region also has numerous underground wine cellars, some of which have been turned into businesses for the benefit of tourists.

The Czech Republic produces burčák, a young fermented wine, which historically and under EU legislation can only be produced from Moravian grapes. It is sweet, golden and cloudy, reminiscent of a juice or soft drink, but still alcoholic in content, between 5 and 8 percent. Burčák is only available on the markets at the start of the grape harvest, between August and November, because it doesn't keep longer than a few weeks.

Slovakia's wine production is mainly in the southern, flatter regions, and the country produces and consumes more wine than the Czechs. Winemaking in

RIGHT Stall selling burčák fermented wine at Zelný Trh market square, in Brno, the Czech Republic.

Slovakia dates back to the seventh century BC – while it is not distributed widely internationally, in large part because its quality development was halted during the Communist regime, it remains a popular choice in Slovakia and its neighbouring countries.

Spirits

An authentic, and mostly homemade, spirit is slivovice (Czech) or slivovica (Slovak), akin to a plum brandy, along with the Slovak juniper berry brandy

ABOVE LEFT Wine tasting at the Národný Salón Vin (the Slovak National Collection of Wine) in Pezinok, Slovakia.

ABOVE RIGHT Vineyard in the autumn, in Moravia, the Czech Republic.

called borovička, a white- or pale-coloured alcohol which is similar to gin. Because these spirits are homemade, the quality and strength varies greatly. The branded, shop-bought products are usually 40 percent alcoholic volume, which is quite weak as far as Czechs and Slovaks are concerned. Pálinka, a fruit distillate, gives the crude product for these spirits, and can be made from any fruit, sometimes potatoes, but plum is the most common. The best pálinka is matured, usually for three years in oak barrels. These spirits are guaranteed to be present at any celebration, festival or party.

Absinthe is legally sold in both countries. This emerald green spirit has a very high alcohol by volume content, up to 80 percent. Another popular liqueur is Czech becherovka, a herbal drink made with a secret recipe of some 34 herbs and 38 percent alcoholic volume. There is a widespread belief that it aids digestion.

Festivals & traditions

The Czechs and Slovaks take great pleasure in their food and many traditional dishes form an integral part of the festivals, celebrations and religious holidays that take place throughout the year. Each one has associated food traditions involving cooking, eating and drinking, as well as other diversions and entertainments such as dressing up, dancing, singing and enjoying the community spirit of public get-togethers. Some of the main highlights of the festival year are mentioned here, from the street parties on New Year's Eve to the autumn wine and beer festivals that would originally have celebrated the end of the hop and grape harvests.

New Year's Eve (Silvestr)

Celebrations at New Year involve loud street parties with bonfires and merrymaking. A great deal of food is made for the festivities, and meat and traditional delicacies are a significant part of the food agenda. The prepared food allows for plenty of visitors, and includes little bread canapés, and plenty of left-overs. For a New Year's Day meal you might find roast goose with sauerkraut and dumplings or schnitzels with potato salad.

Shrovetide (Fašiangy)

Fašiangy, the pre-Lent celebration in Slovakia, takes place in February. With its origins in the Middle Ages, this is an eccentric series of parades, outrageous costumes, songs and dances. Tables are laden with food and alcohol, including whisky, brandy, wine and beer. A more ancient alcoholic drink was medovina, made from fermented honey. Dishes would include baked meat, a pork jelly called bravčová huspenina, fried doughnuts or šišky, smoked bacon or potato fritters.

Easter (Velikonoce and Velka' Noc)

Both countries get thoroughly into the spirit of Easter. The house is given a spring clean and is elaborately furnished with bright, colourful decorations (green, yellow and red), including chicks and lambs. Easter Monday is celebrated with a table loaded with food including canapés, cold meats, cheese and roast lamb or roast goose, and baked sweets such as koláče (sweet buns), a baked ram or beránek (a sweet cake baked in a mould in the shape of a lamb). The sweet Easter breads, mazanec and paška, are served for breakfast or after the meal, presented with a cross on top. In Slovakia and some parts of the Czech Republic, boys wake up on Easter Monday, visit their neighbours and douse the young girls with buckets of water, whipping them (gently on the legs) with woven birch and willow sticks. This is said to bring the girls good health and allow them to stay young.

BELOW LEFT Saint Nicholas, the devil and the angel visiting a Czech cottage.

BELOW CENTRE A Slovak artisan in folk dress shows the art of embroidery at a folk festival in Reidova.

BELOW Decorated eggs are a prominent symbol of Easter in both countries.

RIGHT The Christmas market in Wenceslas Square, Prague, Czech Republic.

In return, the boys are given coloured hardboiled eggs dyed red using hot water, vinegar and onion skins. Nowadays, gifts of chocolate Easter eggs are used. Older men visit their neighbours and receive a shot of plum brandy in return for a blessing before they move on to the next house.

Witches Night (Paleni Čarodějnic)

On 30 April, Czechs collect around a bonfire and burn a figure of a witch who represents winter. The belief was that this would see off the last of the cold weather. Sausages are roasted on sticks, guitars are played and songs sung. When darkness arrives, the witch is brought out, held up and cast on the bonfire.

Summer and autumn folk festivals

Both countries are rich in folk culture despite attempts during the Communist era to reduce the celebrations. Festivals take place in summer and autumn and are full of dancing, traditional costumes, drinking, singing and feasting. The folk dress is elaborate and colourful and often takes a long time to put on (especially for the girls).

Wine and harvest festivals

The regions in the Czech Republic and Slovakia that produce wine (Moravia and the Southern regions of Slovakia) hold festivals, merry occasions with dancing and feasting during September harvest time. Vineyards in the region also welcome visitors to see the wine-making process and buy some bottles.

Food harvest festivals happen during the autumn. One, Posvícení, takes place in church, to thank God for the food harvest, and the other, Obžínky, to celebrate the completion of the harvest. There are various folklore customs associated with this, such as giving the last harvested sheaf of grain to a couple at their marriage ceremony, to bless them with fertility and healthy children.

Saint Nicholas Day (Mikuláš)

This falls on 5 December, celebrating the saint that inspired Santa Claus. If you go out in the evening you may encounter three costumed characters, St Nicholas, an angel and a devil. They are there to find out if children have been good throughout the year – good children are rewarded with sweets and it is said that bad children will be put in the devil's sack.

Christmas (Vánoce and Vianoce)

Celebrated on 24 December, this day used to be spent fasting until dinnertime, but the custom now is to avoid meat until the main evening meal. An elaborate dinner is prepared and this takes up the grand majority of the day. Everyone sits down to eat after sunset, traditionally after the first star comes out.

In Slovakia, the Christmas meal starts with a rich sauerkraut soup (kapustnica), a vegetarian version of the everyday alternative. Before the soup is served (and the rest of the dinner) the family shares a Christmas communion bread called oplatky (Czech) and oblátky (Slovak) that is dipped in honey. Parts of the Czech Republic also serve sauerkraut soup, but this is usually for families with Slovakian roots. Other parts of the Czech Republic serve a fish soup. Carp fried in breadcrumbs with potato salad is the festive dish for the main course. The carp scales symbolize money and wealth, and these would be put under the tablecloth.

After-dinner presents are opened and leftover food and sweets are enjoyed. A sweet bread called vánočka (Czech) and vianočka (Slovak) is another delicacy, eaten on its own or spread with butter and jam, and this is often eaten for breakfast over Christmas. The family will then attend the midnight mass.

Wintertime pig slaughter (Zabijačka and Bravčovina)

Butchering a pig would form a feast day, with the gathering of families to help in the skilful processing of almost all parts of the pig. The supplies would last the family through the cold months of winter. While pig slaughter is less common today, classic pork products are still available, such as tlačenka (brawn), jitrnice (blood sausage) and škvarky (pork crackling).

Name days

Each day of the year is assigned a name in both countries. These names would traditionally have been given to children. Small presents are given to the person whose name day it is, maybe a card and a toast to their health. Some are occasions for a national holiday, such as Václav (St Wenceslas Day) in the Czech Republic.

Classic ingredients

The populations of the Czech Republic and Slovakia are practised at surviving using their land resources, despite the fact that these have certain limitations. The mild climate, with warm summers and long, cold winters, means that fresh vegetables are in short supply. With no sea coasts, only freshwater fish are available, and forests provide game during the hunting season only. So it is left to farmlands to produce the staples of the diet – potatoes, milk, cheese, livestock, wheat, fruit and root vegetables. There are many sheep farms, and this means that milk, cheese and butter are all major players in the cuisines.

Domestic self-sufficiency

In the past, many households owned land that they farmed for profit, but this is now compromised by supermarkets offering vast choices and competitive prices. However, it is still common for country households to have their own small plot of land attached to their house, or in the land adjacent to their town, with a small amount of produce, usually fruit trees and seasonal vegetables, only for their own use, and the joy of growing their own produce.

Hops

Because hops are a principal ingredient in the production of beer, growing them is a rich asset to these two countries. The hops produced are unique to the pale lager, pilsner, that both countries excel at producing – these are the noble hop variety, which is produced for its low bitterness and strong aroma.

Cereals and grains

This food group plays a large part in both cuisines. Bread is eaten for breakfast, as an accompaniment to main courses and as a light snack and dinner. Traditionally rye flour is used in sourdough breadmaking.

Other grains such as rice are popular and are frequently used in more elaborate recipes, such as roulades and stuffed peppers and cabbage, as opposed to just being served as a side dish, although some sauces are perfect served with rice. Pearl barley is used in soup and in preparing pork dishes like black pudding.

There are three traditional types of white flour used in everyday cooking, characterized by the coarseness of the grind: fine white flour (hladká mouka/ múka) for baking and cooking, medium grind (polohrubá mouka/múka) for dumplings and some baking, and coarse grind (hrubá mouka/múka) for making pasta. If you can't get hold of hladká then use plain (all-purpose) flour; substitute polohrubá with half plain (all-purpose)

BELOW LEFT Noble hops growing in the Czech Republic – hops can grow to 6.5m (25ft) so need vertical support

BELOW Flour is graded by coarseness rather than gluten content: polohrubá mouka is medium, hladká mouka is fine, and hrubá mouka is coarse.

flour and half semolina; and hrubá with a third plain (all-purpose) flour and two-thirds semolina. Then there is rye flour, which is used for breadmaking.

Vegetables

Both the Czechs and the Slovaks have extensive areas of arable land, which is used for growing vegetables and fruits. Popular vegetables include gherkins and potatoes, and other root vegetables such as carrots, parsnips and celeriac.

Like many other Eastern European countries, cabbage is a widespread crop that lasts well and is extremely versatile, used in cooking traditional meals and in preparing salads. It is commonly preserved as sauerkraut by pickling, where it is finely chopped, seasoned with salt, and allowed to mature and ferment in oak barrels. The traditional way of preparing the cabbage was in a large oak basin, where it would be stepped on with bare feet to allow the juices to come out and to tenderize the leaves. Sauerkraut keeps for up to seven months, and was stored and used during the cold winter period, but nowadays it is so readily available that it is a popular ingredient in modern cooking. It is usually served as an accompaniment to meat dishes, often pork, with potatoes or dumplings. A simpler dish might involve sauerkraut and Czech or Slovak sausage.

The abundance of forests in both countries have made mushrooms a

ABOVE Potatoes, carrots, parsnips and celeriac are root vegetables that can be harvested in the autumn and are available throughout the winter.

ABOVE RIGHT Nuts are a significant part of the produce of both countries and walnuts, especially, feature frequently in the cuisine.

popular ingredient and hunting for them a common pastime. This is a frequent holiday pursuit for familes when camping or on holiday. Most people who pick mushrooms are well educated in the dangers and in recognizing poisonous types. Typical dishes with this ingredient include mushroom soup and fried scrambled mushrooms with an egg and mushroom sauce.

Nuts

Many nuts, usually finely chopped, are used in the baking of cakes and pastries, especially walnuts, which are grown in both countries. Other varieties such as almonds and hazelnuts appear in some traditional recipes, but due to their higher cost they are less popular.

Pulses

Beans, peas and lentils are all examples of pulses that are central to both cuisines, generally dried ones that require at least a day's soaking. There are many more varieties of pulses available now and these are often used in soups and thick sauces.

Fresh Carrot Salad
(Jablkovo-mrkvový šalát/salát)

This refreshing side salad can accompany many main meals, especially fried dishes.

Serves 4

8 carrots, finely grated
2 sweet apples, peeled and
   finely grated
juice of ½ lemon, strained
15g/1oz/1 tbsp icing
   (confectioner's) sugar (optional)
a handful of dried sultanas
   (golden raisins) (optional)
a handful of fresh chunks of
   pineapple (optional)

Combine the carrots, apples and sultanas and pineapple, if using. Add the lemon juice and icing sugar to taste. Serve in a little bowl.

PER SERVING: Energy 170kcal/720kj; Protein 2g; Carbohydrate 41g, of which sugars 40g; Fat 1g, of which saturates 0g; Cholesterol 0mg; Calcium 69mg; Fibre 7.7g; Sodium 56mg.

Fruits and berries

There is a large selection of fruit crops in the Czech Republic and Slovakia, including apples, pears, apricots, plums, peaches, cherries and figs. These are popularly preserved in jams, marmalades and compôtes and are used in cooking and baking. The same applies to the vast array of berries, including strawberries, raspberries, blueberries, gooseberries and redcurrants.

Dairy

There is a wide range of dairy products unique to each country and integral to the cuisines. This is partly because of the importance of self-sufficiency during past wars and occupations, as well as the commerical potential of the products.

The volume of farmed sheep and cattle ensures an active cheese-making industry. Slovak bryndza cheese is made from sheep's milk and is one of the most traditional and commonly used ingredients in its cuisine. A popular accompaniment to bryndza dishes is soured milk (acidofilné mlieko) and kefír, traditional drinks created to make the most efficient use of the fresh produce in a farming culture. The notable cheese from the Czech Republic is Hermelín, similar to the French soft cheeses, Camembert and Brie.

Cow's milk is often used in cooking. Yogurt, hard cheese, soft cheese, curd cheese (tvaroh), cream and sour cream are all easily found. Tvaroh is a curd cheese popular in both countries,

ABOVE, FROM LEFT TO RIGHT Apricots are one of many stone fruits grown in the Czech Republic and Slovakia; Povidla (Czech) and Lekvár (Slovak) is a thick jam, and vanilkový cukr is vanilla essence powder; Tvaroh (curd cheese), is widely used in cooking – it can be substituted with Quark cheese.

mainly in sweet dishes, often mixed with icing sugar, and made into sweet snacks for children.

Kefír is a fermented milk drink with a thick yogurt-like consistency. It is drunk in the same way as milk and is considered extremely healthy, supporting the immune and digestive systems. Sour milk, as opposed to fresh milk, is left to ferment and acquires a distinctive sour taste.

Plum Jam (Švestkové povidla/Slivkový lekvár)

This thick spread has a texture like plum stew, and is often used in Czech and Slovak pastries and cakes. It can be hard to source elsewhere so this recipe will be handy.

Makes about 2kg/4½lbs
4kg/9lb plums, pitted
800g/1¾lb/4 cups caster (superfine) sugar
60ml/4 tbsp white vinegar

1 Preheat the oven to 200°C/400°F/Gas 6. Cut the plums into bite-sized pieces and put into a bowl. Add the sugar and vinegar, and mix thoroughly.

2 Transfer to a baking dish. Bake for 20 minutes, or until the plums boil.

3 Reduce the temperature to 140°C/275°F/Gas 1 and bake for 4 hours, stirring every 30 minutes. Remove and cool. Spoon into jam jars. Seal. The plum jam will last for up to 3 months without preserving.

PER SERVING: Energy 230kcal/985kj; Protein 1g; Carbohydrate 60g, of which sugars 60g; Fat 0g, of which saturates 0g; Cholesterol 0mg; Calcium 30mg; Fibre 4.6g; Sodium 6mg.

Fish

Freshwater fish are caught domestically in the many rivers across the Czech Republic and Slovakia. The two most popular fish are carp and trout, the former often consumed for a traditional Christmas dinner.

Meat, poultry and game

The Czechs and Slovaks both love their meat. Pork and beef are often stewed, roasted, fried, and poultry is often roasted whole, especially duck and goose for special occasions. The preparation of the meat is invariably minimal, with the flavours brought out in an accompanying sauce or complementary vegetable such as sauerkraut. Oven roasting is the most popular form of cooking meat.

Rabbit used to be a common menu speciality, because households would invariably keep rabbits in their gardens. However this is no longer the case, and while still featuring in the cuisine, rabbit is now much less popular than 20 years ago.

BELOW, FROM LEFT TO RIGHT Sausages, or klobása, include jíternice and jelita, offal sausages from the Czech Republic, and Slovak klobása, similar to bratwurst, but less juicy and more peppery; ketchup is sweeter and less dense than in other parts of Europe; lard and fat are now less used, but still feature to give extra flavour.

Lamb is an expensive meat and is considered a delicacy, most frequently prepared for a special Easter meal.

Game, due to the vast woods and forests, is a popular and common autumn delicacy. Game meat is usually marinated before cooking, as it is an aromatic meat and can sometimes be overpowering. The most popular hunted animals include wild boar, deer (venison) and pheasant.

The most used type of bacon is smoked streaky bacon. This is often diced and fried, then used as topping for meatless dishes. It is also used to fill other types of meats or offered as a cold appetizer, accompanied with bread.

Sauces

Usually made with a butter and flour base, cream and vegetables, sauces form a significant part of each cuisine. Not only do they accompany most meat and dumpling dishes, but they are served in a large quantity, often 2–3 ladlefuls per serving.

Ketchup and mustard

Czech and Slovak ketchup is much sweeter, more watery and lighter than other varieties. There are two kinds of mustard, horseradish flavoured and full fat. The horseradish version has a bit more kick to it, while the full-fat one is quite mild. Full-fat mustard is often used to flavour sauces and meat.

Spices, flavourings and herbs

The simplicity of both cuisines is evident in the minimal use of spices and exotic flavourings. The most common and popular seasonings are salt, pepper, caraway, dill, paprika, marjoram and vegeta. These give the dishes quite distinctive natural flavours based on the wholesome goodness of the ingredients.

Vegeta is a food seasoning, a mixture of vegetables and seasoning herbs, and this often replaces the use of salt and pepper in recipes, and is also used in seasoning soup and meat.

The fresh herbs used in Czech and Slovak cooking include parsley, dill, thyme, chives, and even stinging nettles. Vinegar is often used to marinate, flavour and preserve foods. The most traditional is white distilled 8 percent vinegar.

The liquid seasoning Maggi is a dark sauce, made of hydrolyzed vegetable protein. Like salt and pepper, it is always on the dining table, and is used to season soup as well as salads and sauces. It can be substituted with soy sauce.

Lard and fat

Pork lard, goose and duck fat were frequently used in cooking, frying and baking, but have recently been replaced by healthier alternatives such as sunflower, vegetable and olive oil. Some of the most authentic dishes benefit from the use of lard and fat, as they add considerable flavour.

SOUPS

Main meals in the Czech Republic and Slovakia are traditionally eaten at lunchtime. They consist of two or more courses, and the first one is always soup. Because this dish is such an everyday feature of the family table, the Czechs and Slovaks have become masters of teasing out every kind of flavour and taste from their soups. The ingredients used are those that are easily sourced locally – root vegetables, beans, any available meat, and garlic, paprika, bay leaves and marjoram to spice things up.

Light broths to thick goulash soups

Choices for the soup course are varied. Light options include the classic broth, Beef Broth with Dumplings, a simple dish served with rich, meaty dumplings, and a popular choice at wedding receptions and other special occasions. Chicken soup, or here Chicken Noodle Soup, is another delicate soup favoured in the Czech Republic and Slovakia, and both countries use parsley root to make it – this looks just like a small carrot, but is a white colour. Thick vegetable soups are another Eastern European favourite, made with combinations of peas, beans, lentils, potatoes, mushrooms, corn on the cob, carrots or other locally grown ingredients.

Originating from neighbouring Hungary, Goulash Soup (Gulášová polévka/Gulášová polievka) is a thick, spicy, meat-based soup. Typically prepared with beef, veal, pork or lamb, it is often served with tiny egg noodles (nudle/rezance), with the meat gently browned and the vegetable ingredients left to simmer alongside the meat on the stove, allowing the flavours to mingle. This soup is very substantial and filling, and is therefore often used as the main dish of the day, perhaps then followed by a lighter sweet course.

Another meaty option is Black Pudding Soup (Zabijačková polévka/Zabijačková), one of many offal dishes that reflect the strong farming economy, where families needed to make use of every part of a slaughtered animal, including the stomach lining. These soups have a dense consistency and are said to be an acquired taste, but their mild, meaty flavour is also appreciated as a cosseting, warming treat.

In the modern age, soup has become less of an essential daily sustenance and more of a comfort food, with various soup dishes favoured because they reflect a nostalgia for past mealtime traditions.

Most of the classic soup recipes shown here have a thickening, which consists simply of oil and flour, although often with fried onions included. It is important to cook the flour in the oil for 2–3 minutes, long enough so it is digestible, and then to add it to the soup at just the right temperature so that it does not curdle.

Serves 3–4

300g/11oz/1⅔ cups haricot (navy) beans, soaked overnight and drained

2 bay leaves

1 garlic clove, peeled and crushed

45ml/3 tbsp tomato purée (paste)

1 vegetable stock (bouillon) cube

1–2 potatoes, peeled and diced

2 x Polish or Hungarian sausages or 150g/5oz smoked bacon, chopped (optional)

5ml/1 tsp salt

1 onion, peeled and finely chopped

50ml/2fl oz/¼ cup vegetable or sunflower oil

15ml/1 tbsp plain (all-purpose) flour

45ml/3 tbsp white vinegar

5ml/1 tsp sugar

200ml/7fl oz/scant 1 cup double (heavy) cream (optional)

crusty bread, to serve

Sour Bean Soup
Fazulová polévka/Fazuľová polievka

This is a very hearty Slovak recipe consisting of basic ingredients from the pantry. The soup would have been made of small haricot beans, but you can also use kidney beans or a mixture of the two.

1 Put the beans in a large pan with 1.5 litres/2½ pints/6¼ cups cold water. Add the bay leaves, crushed garlic, tomato purée and the vegetable stock cube. Bring to the boil and cook for 30 minutes.

2 Add the potatoes (and sausage or bacon, if using) to the soup and cook for a further 30 minutes, or until the beans and potatoes are soft. Add 5ml/1 tsp salt.

3 Meanwhile, when the beans are almost cooked, fry the onions in the oil until they are golden. Add the flour and cook for 2–4 minutes over low heat, until the mixture is golden.

4 Take the soup off the heat and add the onion mixture, stirring well. Add the vinegar, sugar and cream, if using, and simmer for 5 minutes. Serve.

COOK'S TIP

You can use canned beans, but rinse them thoroughly. This will eliminate the soaking time and reduce the cooking time to 30–45 minutes.

PER SERVING: Energy 780kcal/3523kj; Protein 30g; Carbohydrate 53g, of which sugars 9g; Fat 51g, of which saturates 22g; Cholesterol 102mg; Calcium 183mg; Fibre 18.4g; Sodium 1832mg.

Serves 3–4

250g/9oz/generous 1 cup green lentils, soaked for 3–4 hours and drained
1 vegetable stock (bouillon) cube
2 carrots, peeled and chopped
25g/1oz/2 tbsp butter
1 medium onion, peeled and chopped
45ml/3 tbsp plain (all-purpose) flour
2–3 garlic cloves, peeled and crushed
10ml/2 tsp marjoram

For the dumplings
150g/5oz/1¼ cups plain (all-purpose) flour
1 egg
30ml/2 tbsp milk
pinch of salt and ground black pepper

Lentil Soup with Dumplings
Čočková polévka s knedlíčky/ Šošovicová polievka s knedlíčkami

Green lentils are the only lentil used in traditional Czech and Slovak cooking. They have a meaty flavour and combine well with these simple dumplings.

COOK'S TIP
A runny dough is required for the dumplings so they are light and fluffy.

1 Put the lentils in a pan with 1.5 litres/2½ pints/6¼ cups water. Add the stock cube and the carrots, and cook for 30 minutes over medium heat, until almost soft.

2 To make dumplings, mix the flour, egg, milk, and seasoning. Add a few tablespoons of cold water to make a sticky, fairly runny dough – so that you can almost pour it into the soup.

3 When the lentils are almost cooked, heat the butter in a pan, add the onion and fry for 5–10 minutes, or until golden. Add the flour and cook over low heat for 2–3 minutes.

4 Remove the soup from the heat and gradually add the hot flour mixture, stirring constantly. Return the soup to the heat, and add the garlic and marjoram with salt to taste.

5 Using a fork and spoon, roughly mould the dough into balls and drop into the boiling soup. Cook for 10–15 minutes (the dumplings will rise to the surface when cooked).

PER SERVING: Energy 465kcal/1965kj; Protein 23g; Carbohydrate 76g, of which sugars 8g; Fat 9g, of which saturates 4g; Cholesterol 72mg; Calcium 165mg; Fibre 3.6g; Sodium 380mg.

Garlic Soup
Česnečka/Cesnaková polievka

This hearty dish is traditional in the Czech Republic, and probably the simplest to make of all their soups. It is believed to be a remedy for the common cold as well as an excellent cure for a hangover.

Serves 3–4

500g/1¼lb waxy potatoes, peeled and diced
5ml/1 tsp caraway seeds or ground caraway (optional)
2 beef or vegetable stock (bouillon) cubes
15ml/1 tbsp butter
1 egg, beaten
4 garlic cloves, peeled and crushed
5ml/1 tsp dried marjoram
salt and ground black pepper

For the garnish

15ml/1 tbsp butter for frying
2–3 slices of rye bread, cut into small croûtons
50g/2oz Camembert or Brie, rind removed, cut into four pieces (optional)
a little chopped fresh parsley, to garnish

1 Put the potatoes into a large pan with 1.5 litres/2½ pints/6¼ cups water, together with 5ml/1 tsp salt and the caraway. Bring the pan to the boil and cook for 15–20 minutes, or until the potatoes are soft.

2 Add the stock cubes and butter, then simmer for 2 minutes. Pour the egg into the soup and leave to cook for 2 minutes.

3 Mix the garlic with the marjoram and a pinch of salt. Add to the soup with black pepper, and cook for a few more minutes.

4 Heat the butter for the garnish in a frying pan and add the rye bread. Fry until golden and crispy, to make croûtons. These can be left to cool down and dry out even more. Serve the soup hot, with chopped fresh parsley and the croûtons.

COOK'S TIPS

• To make this recipe friendlier on the waistline, omit the butter, and garnish with parsley, or the bread can be toasted instead of fried.
• If you like, add a spoonful of soft cheese such as camembert before serving.

PER SERVING: Energy 201kcal/1843kj; Protein 2g; Carbohydrate 54g, of which sugars 9g; Fat 43g, of which saturates 26g; Cholesterol 107mg; Calcium 125mg; Fibre 10.8g; Sodium 781mg.

Serves 3–4

30ml/2 tbsp dried champignon
  mushrooms
200g/7oz butter
1 onion, peeled and diced
2 carrots, peeled and diced
¼ celeriac root, peeled and diced
1 leek, chopped
salt and ground black pepper
1.5 litres/2½ pints/6¼ cups water
500g/1¼lb potatoes, peeled and cut into
  cubes
1 meat or vegetarian stock (bouillon) cube
1 bay leaf
3 garlic cloves, peeled and thinly sliced
115g/4oz/1 cup plain (all-purpose) flour
10ml/2 tsp dried marjoram
leaves from 3 parsley sprigs, to garnish
bread, to serve

Potato Soup

Bramborová polévka/Zemiaková polievka

This is a classic vegetable winter warmer in the
Czech Republic and Slovakia. Potatoes and other root
vegetables are incorporated in all kinds of recipes
because they are inexpensive and easily available.

1 Soak the dried mushrooms in
water to cover for about 20 minutes
before you begin cooking.

2 Melt half the butter in a large pan
and gently fry the onion, carrots,
celeriac and leek for 5–10 minutes
or until they are light golden. Add
salt and pepper, and 1.5 litres /2½
pints/6¼ cups of boiling water.

3 Drain the mushrooms, reserving
the liquor. Add the mushrooms to the
soup and strain in the liquor.

4 Add the potatoes, stock cube, bay
leaf and garlic. Bring to the boil and
simmer for 20–30 minutes, or until
the potatoes are soft.

5 Melt the remaining butter in a
small pan and add the flour. Cook for
2–3 minutes, stirring constantly, then
add to the soup, stirring constantly.
Add the marjoram and cook for
another 5 minutes. Garnish with
parsley leaves and serve with bread.

VARIATION

You can also add the florets from half a
head of cauliflower, if you like.

PER SERVING: Energy 629kcal/2616kj; Protein 9g; Carbohydrate 54g, of which sugars 9g; Fat 43g, of which saturates 26g; Cholesterol 107mg; Calcium125mg; Fibre 10.8g; Sodium 781mg.

Serves 4

1 small chicken
1.5 litres/2½ pints/6¼ cups water
1 onion, cut into wedges
1 carrot, peeled and sliced
1 parsnip, peeled and sliced
1 leek, white parts only, cut into chunks
5ml/1 tsp salt
45ml/3 tbsp finely chopped parsley,
   to garnish
60ml/4 tbsp smetana or crème fraîche,
   to serve

For the noodles

150g/5oz/1¼ cups plain white
   (all-purpose) flour
1 egg
30–45ml/2–3 tbsp cold water
1.5ml/¼ tsp salt

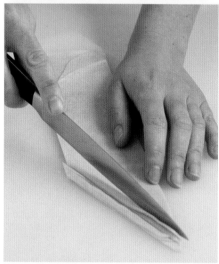

Chicken Noodle Soup
Slepiči vývar/Slepači vývar

The stock for this soup should be as clear as a teardrop.
Only half the noodles are required, so keep the rest in an
airtight container in the refrigerator for up to a week.

1 Put the chicken in a large pan,
add the water and bring to the boil.
Then simmer for 5 minutes. Skim the
surface. Add the onion, carrot, parsnip,
leek and salt to the pan, cover and
simmer over a low-medium heat for
45 minutes, until the chicken is tender.

2 Using a slotted spoon, remove the
vegetables from the pan and discard
them. Transfer the chicken to a
plate, put aside and leave to cool.
Pass the stock through a sieve
(strainer) and pour back into the pan.
When the chicken is cool, cut into
bitesize pieces.

3 To make the noodles, put the flour,
egg, water and salt in a processor
and blend to a smooth dough.

4 Put the dough on a floured surface
and knead for 2–3 minutes. Wrap in
clear film (plastic wrap) and leave to
rest in the refrigerator for 30 minutes.

5 Divide the dough into four pieces.
Using a rolling pin or pasta machine,
roll out each piece until very thin, and
then cut into 5–6cm/2–2½in strips.
Leave to dry for 5 minutes. Place a
few strips on top of each other and
shred them diagonally into very thin
strips. Toss in flour and allow to dry.

6 Put the chicken pieces into four
serving bowls. Bring the stock to the
boil, add half the noodles and cook
for 5 minutes. Pour into the bowls,
garnish with chopped parsley.

PER SERVING: Energy 427kcal/1805kJ; Protein 54.5g; Carbohydrate 40.2g, of which sugars 7.8g; Fat 6.4g, of which saturates 1.7g; Cholesterol 152mg; Calcium 76mg; Fibre 5.3g; Sodium 237mg.

Serves 3–4

500g/1¼lb beef shin or leg (shank)
1 onion, unpeeled, ends cut off
5ml/1 tsp salt
1 garlic clove, unpeeled, ends cut off
1 bay leaf
8 whole peppercorns
2 carrots, tops removed
1 celery stick
1–2 parsley stalks
150g/5oz extra-fine noodles (optional)
parsley, to garnish

For the liver dumplings

400g/14oz beef or pork liver
15ml/1 tbsp fresh chopped marjoram
30ml/2 tbsp butter
1 egg
½ garlic clove, peeled and crushed
3–4 parsley sprigs, leaves chopped
salt and ground black pepper
200g/7oz dry breadcrumbs

Beef Broth with Dumplings
Hovězí vývar s játrovými knedlíčky/ Hovädzí vývar s pečeňovými knedlíčky

This rich broth would traditionally be made from bones, and when meat was used the soup would be served with the main dish. Here, liver dumplings are served with the soup.

1 Put the beef into a large pan or pressure cooker with 2.5 litres/4¼ pints of water. Add the onion, salt, garlic, bay leaf, peppercorns, carrots, celery and parsley. Cook for 4–5 hours in a pan, or for 2 hours in a pressure cooker, until the meat is tender. You may need to top up the water in the pan – there should be enough to cover the meat.

2 Mince (grind) or scrape the liver until fine. Add the marjoram, butter, egg, garlic, parsley and seasoning. Mix and thicken with the breadcrumbs.

3 Add the breadcrumbs to bind the dough but don't add so many that it crumbles. Using a tablespoon, scoop bits of the dough and mould into a round ball with a diameter of 5cm/2in.

4 Lift the meat from the broth and set aside (use this to serve with your main course). Run the remaining liquid and vegetables through a sieve, leaving just broth. (Then blend the vegetables and add cream to make a sauce.)

5 Drop in the dumplings and cook for 5–10 minutes. Test whether they are cooked through by cutting one open (the actual cooking time will depend on the size of your dumplings).

6 Prepare the noodles according to the packet instructions – usually they need to be covered with boiling water for 3 minutes. Leave in a separate serving dish. Serve the broth with 2–3 dumplings per portion and 2 tablespoons of noodles. Garnish with fresh parsley.

PER SERVING: Energy 412kcal/1730kj; Protein 29g; Carbohydrate 39g, of which sugars 1g; Fat 7g, of which saturates 7g; Cholesterol 344mg; Calcium 87mg; Fibre 2.8g; Sodium 881mg.

Serves 3–4

1 onion, peeled and finely chopped

45ml/3 tbsp oil

400g/14oz stewing beef, cut into
  2cm/¾in cubes

1 tbsp ground red paprika

1.5 litres/2½ pints/6¼ cups boiling water

2 beef stock (bouillon) cubes

3 potatoes, peeled and diced

50g/2oz/½ cup plain (all-purpose) flour

10ml/2 tsp dried marjoram

5ml/1 tsp ground black pepper

30ml/2 tbsp tomato purée (paste)

5 garlic cloves, peeled and crushed

salt

fresh chopped parsley, to garnish

rye bread, rohlíky, or rožky, to serve

VARIATION

To make a much cheaper version of this recipe, use frankfurters instead of beef. Rather than cooking the potatoes separately, cook these first and add all the ingredients to the potato pan.

Goulash Soup
Gulášová polévka/Gulášová polievka

This classic soup has many variations, found across both countries. Many of these might use a frankfurter sausage instead of beef, with the base of the soup being potatoes, a low-cost ingredient. This recipe, though, uses beef cooked until it is meltingly tender.

1 Using a large pan, gently fry the onion in the oil for 5–10 minutes or until golden. Add the beef cubes and season with 5ml/1 tsp salt.

2 Add the paprika and fry for 1 minute, taking care not to burn the paprika, which would make it bitter.

3 Pour over the boiling water and add the stock cubes. Cook over medium heat for 45 minutes to 1 hour, or until the meat is tender. Meanwhile, boil the potatoes in another pan for 15–20 minutes, or until tender.

4 In a small bowl, mix the flour with 15ml/1 tbsp cold water and, when the meat is cooked, stir this into the soup.

5 Add the cooked potatoes, marjoram, black pepper, tomato purée and garlic. Taste and adjust the seasoning to your preference, then cook for a further 5 minutes. Garnish with chopped parsley and serve with rye bread, rohlíky or rožky.

PER SERVING: Energy 313kcal/1314kj; Protein 11g; Carbohydrate 29g, of which sugars 2g; Fat 24g, of which saturates 10g; Cholesterol 51mg; Calcium128mg; Fibre 1.3g; Sodium 433mg.

Serves 4

50g/2oz pearl barley
400g black pudding (blood sausages)
2 garlic cloves, peeled and crushed
5ml/1 tsp marjoram
1 onion, peeled and finely chopped
15ml/1 tbsp pork fat, butter or oil
ground black pepper
rye bread, to serve

Black Pudding Soup
Zabijačková polévka/Zabijačková polievka

This soup is a delicacy in the Czech Republic. Traditionally, it would only be made once a year when it was time to slaughter the family pig (most families in rural households would have owned one). The whole family would come together to help, and in return everyone would carry away a share of the day's produce. Meat from a pig would last the family a long time, and was kept chilled in an enormous storage freezer.

1 Bring 2 litres/3½ pints/9 cups water to the boil in a large pan and add 2.5ml/½ tsp salt. Add the barley and cook for about 45 minutes, or according to the packet instructions, until soft.

2 Remove the skin from the black pudding and mash the sausage with a fork. Add to the barley, with the garlic, marjoram and a little pepper. Cook for a further 10 minutes.

3 Meanwhile, fry the onion in the fat, butter or oil for 5–10 minutes, or until golden. Add to the soup. Serve with rye bread.

COOK'S TIP
For the truly adventurous, replace some of the water with up to 300ml/½ pint/1¼ cups of pig's blood – just sieve it and add to the soup after the barley is cooked.

PER SERVING: Energy 366kcal/1526kj; Protein 11g; Carbohydrate 29g, of which sugars 2g; Fat 24g, of which saturates 10g; Cholesterol 51mg; Calcium128mg; Fibre 1.3g; Sodium 953mg.

Sauerkraut Soup
Zelnačka/Kapustnica

This is a traditional Slovak dish, and one that is guaranteed to remind Slovak people of home when they are abroad. As is often the case, there are different variations of the dish. Slovakians prepare this soup throughout the year, and sauerkraut is one of the most common ingredients, but they like to vary the dish by adding more meat, and perhaps adding pulses such as haricot beans.

Serves 3–4

approximately 300g/11oz smoked pork knuckle (size can vary)
1 whole allspice berry
5 whole black peppercorns
5ml/1 tsp caraway seeds
1 bay leaf
400g/14oz sauerkraut, juice reserved
1 onion, peeled and finely chopped
65ml/4½ tbsp oil
10ml/2 tsp paprika
100g/3¾oz/1¾ cups dried mushrooms
2 garlic cloves, peeled and crushed
1 large Slovak sausage 'klobasa'
    (alternatively use Polish or Hungarian)
5ml/1 tsp sugar
15ml/1 tbsp white vinegar
5ml/1 tsp dried marjoram
45ml/3 tbsp plain (all-purpose) flour
salt
sour cream or natural yogurt, to garnish
boiled caraway potatoes or thick-cut rye
    bread, to serve

COOK'S TIP
This soup really gets its flavour and 'kick' when it has been left in the refrigerator for at least one day before serving.

1 Put the pork knuckle in a large pan with 2.5 litres/4 pints/10 cups water, 15ml/1 tbsp salt, the allspice, peppercorns, caraway seeds and bay leaf. Bring to the boil, then simmer for 30 minutes. Add the sauerkraut with half the juice from the jar.

2 In a small pan, fry the onion in 15ml/1 tbsp oil for 5 minutes, or until it is translucent but not brown, then stir in the paprika. Add this to the soup with the mushrooms and garlic. Cook for 30 minutes, or until the meat is thoroughly tender.

3 Lift the knuckle out of the soup, then strip the meat off the bone. Cut or tear it into small pieces and put back into the soup. You can also use a small amount of the skin, but make sure it is cut into very small pieces. Cook for a further 20 minutes.

4 Cut up the sausage and add to the soup with the sugar, vinegar, marjoram and more salt to taste.

5 Heat the remaining oil in a separate pan, add the flour and cook for 2–3 minutes. Take the soup off the hob and add the flour mixture, stirring constantly. Cook for another 5 minutes. Serve garnished with sour cream or yogurt and accompanied by potatoes that have been boiled with some salt and caraway seeds, or with rye bread.

PER SERVING: Energy 222kcal/926kj; Protein 16g; Carbohydrate 18g, of which sugars 6g; Fat 10g, of which saturates 3g; Cholesterol 29mg; Calcium 126mg; Fibre 7.9g; Sodium 935mg.

SNACKS, APPETIZERS & LIGHT MEALS

In this chapter you will find a tempting range of fresh, simply prepared recipes. These are dishes that are characteristic of the way that Czechs and Slovaks tend to dine: a substantial, meat-based lunchtime meal, small snacks throughout the day and then a simple, light evening meal, typically just a single course. Most of the options here, such as Spicy Marinated Cheese or Drowned Sausages, are classic fare in bars, and are glorious served with a glass of cold Czech or Slovak beer.

Dumplings, pickled sausages & salads

Despite their simplicity, many of the recipes in this chapter have rich flavours. While soup is the appetizer of choice (with the options amply covered in the previous chapter), you will find plenty of other ideas here.

Some dishes, such as Cold Cod Salad and Marinated Cheese (nakládany hermelín), using Camembert or the local speciality, hermelín, are good choices for an appetizer, and are also favoured as barside and restaurant snacks, usually accompanied with a pint of beer. Pickled Sausages, with the Czech word for the dish, utopenci, meaning 'drowned men', are soaked in a sweet vinegar marinade with the piquant addition of pepper, onion and chillies. Such light dishes are an essential part of the vibrant bar culture in both countries – it is only the very smallest drinking houses who don't offer food to their customers. Fried Bread with Spicy Stir-fry with pepper, tomatoes and egg is another example of pub fare, or Potato Dumplings with Pork Crackling, served with smoked bacon, sauerkraut, and a sauce of fried onion and sauerkraut juice.

Salads featuring a single vegetable, such as cucumber, tomato, carrot or cabbage, are straightforward to prepare and served customarily as side dishes or light meals. They have become familiar trademark dishes in both countries, almost in the same way as dumplings.

Salads in both countries characteristically have a simple sugar and vinegar base and no dressing, although sometimes include mayonnaise, and they are ideal accompaniments to fried main courses. Because they are full of flavour, have such generous servings and represent a healthy option, salads are also often enjoyed as a main course, including for breakfast when they are usually served with the freshly baked rolls (rohlíky/rožky). In Slovakia, mixed salads (miešaný šalát) can include canned rather than fresh vegetables (sterilizovaný).

With the exception of the dumpling dishes, regional breads such as rye bread and rohlíky (Czech) or rožky (Slovak) (see pages 124–125), would be commonly used as serving accompaniments to meals.

Serves 2

200g/7oz Brie or Camembert
6–10 red chillies (fresh or dried) or
  5–10ml/1–2 tsp chilli powder or
  cayenne pepper, or to taste
1 tsp dried thyme or herbs de provence
15ml/1 tbsp paprika
5ml/1 tsp whole peppercorns
pinch of salt
1 white onion, peeled and cut into long,
  thin strips
1 garlic clove, peeled and cut into slices
3 bay leaves
500ml/17fl oz/2¼ cups sunflower oil
rye bread or topinka, to serve

Spicy Marinated Cheese
Nakládany hermelín

A classic snack in pubs, this dish is perfect with a pint of cold beer. The recipe uses a cheese called hermelín, produced in Czech Bohemia, in a city called Sedlčany, but it can be substituted with Camembert or Brie.

1 Cut the cheese into eight cubes; this will allow the flavours to soak in quickly and penetrate the whole cube of cheese.

2 Mix the cheese in a bowl with the chillies, thyme, paprika, peppercorns and salt. Then add the onion, garlic and bay leaves, and mix together gently.

3 Transfer to a clean jar with a resealable lid and pour in the oil. Cover all the ingredients and tighten the lid. Marinate in the refrigerator for 2 days. Serve with rye bread or topinky (rye bread fried with garlic).

COOK'S TIPS
• You will need a jar with a resealable lid such as a sterilized pickle jar.
• If you are sampling during marinating, don't return the tasting fork or spoon to the jar otherwise you are likely to introduce new bacteria.
• Marinate for 2 days, then keep the dish chilled for up to 7 days, or sooner if you see bubbles start to appear.

PER SERVING: Energy 291kcal/5324kj; Protein 23g; Carbohydrate 9g, of which sugars 5g; Fat 130g, of which saturates 30g; Cholesterol 93mg; Calcium 299mg; Fibre 1.1g; Sodium 766mg.

Serves 6–8

6 large waxy potatoes, peeled
2 eggs, beaten
1–2 garlic cloves, crushed
115g/4oz/1 cup plain flour
5ml/1 tsp chopped fresh marjoram
50g/2oz/4 tbsp butter
60ml/4 tbsp oil
salt and freshly ground black pepper
sour cream, chopped fresh parsley and a
tomato salad, to serve

COOK'S TIP

Put potatoes in water with a few drops of
lemon, to prevent them turning brown.

Potato Pancakes

Bramboráky/Zemiakové placky

These little snacks are popular street food in the
Czech Republic, available at roadside stalls and cafés.
Quick and easy to make, they are a tasty adaptation of
the classic flour-based pancake.

1 Grate the potatoes and squeeze
dry, using a dish towel.

2 Put the potatoes in a bowl with the
eggs, garlic, flour, marjoram and
seasoning and mix well.

3 Heat half the butter and oil
together in a large frying pan then
add large spoonfuls of the potato
mixture to form rounds. Carefully
flatten the pancakes well with the
back of a dampened spoon.

4 Fry the pancakes until they are
crisp and golden brown, then turn
over and cook on the other side.
Drain on kitchen paper and keep
warm while cooking the rest of the
pancakes, adding the remaining
butter and oil to the frying pan
as necessary.

5 Serve the pancakes topped with
soured cream, sprinkled with parsley,
and accompanied by a fresh, juicy
tomato salad.

PER SERVING: Energy 291kcal/1221kJ; Protein 6g; Carbohydrate 35.4g, of which sugars 2.9g; Fat 15g, of which saturates 2.2g; Cholesterol 63mg; Calcium 36mg; Fibre 2.1g; Sodium 42mg.

Serves 4

For the cucumber salad

2 whole cucumbers, peeled
pinch of salt
pinch of ground black pepper
45ml/3 tbsp sugar, or to taste
60ml/4 tbsp white vinegar, or to taste
150ml/¼ pint/⅔ cup sour cream or
    natural (plain) yogurt
3 garlic cloves, peeled and crushed

For the tomato and onion salad

6 tomatoes, sliced
2 onions, peeled and thinly sliced
pinch of salt
pinch of ground black pepper
15ml/1 tbsp sugar, or to taste
30ml/2 tbsp white vinegar, or to taste
200ml/7fl oz/scant 1 cup boiling water

VARIATIONS

• Use natural (plain) yogurt instead of
sour cream for the cucumber salad.
• You can use lemon juice instead of
vinegar for the tomato salad.

Cucumber & Tomato Salads

Okurkový a rajčatový salát/Uhorkový a paradajkový šalát

These two fresh salads, cucumber salad with cream, and tomato and onion salad, will be found on almost any menu in the Czech Republic and Slovakia. They are served as side dishes, the cucumber one a favourite to accompany fried dishes such as schnitzels and fried cheese.

1 To make the cucumber salad, grate the cucumbers coarsely into a bowl. Add salt, pepper, sugar and vinegar, adjusting the quantities of sugar and vinegar to taste.

2 Add the sour cream and crushed garlic to the salad. Then chill in the refrigerator. Serve the dish as a side salad with a fried main course.

1 To make the tomato and onion salad, put the vegetable ingredients in a bowl and add the salt and pepper. In a separate container mix the sugar, vinegar and boiling water, adjusting the sugar and vinegar to taste.

2 Pour the mixture over the salad, then chill in the refrigerator for 1–2 hours. Serve as a side salad for main courses.

CUCUMBER SALAD, PER SERVING: Energy 144kcal/598kj; Protein 3g; Carbohydrate 16g, of which sugars 16g; Fat 8g, of which saturates 5g; Cholesterol 23mg; Calcium 69mg; Fibre 1.2g; Sodium 120mg.
TOMATO SALAD, PER SERVING: Energy 69kcal/292kj; Protein 2g; Carbohydrate 15g, of which sugars 13g; Fat 1g, of which saturates 0g; Cholesterol 0mg; Calcium 31mg; Fibre 3.1g; Sodium 115mg.

Serves 3–4
280ml/9fl oz/1¼ cups white vinegar
30ml/2 tbsp black peppercorns
5 large bay leaves
800g–1kg/1¾–2¼lb cod fillets
2 large carrots, peeled but left whole
2 onions, peeled and finely chopped
50–80g/2–3oz/¼–⅓ cup mayonnaise
salt
5ml/1 tsp ground black pepper
fresh white rolls or rohlíky/rožky, to serve

Cold Cod Salad
Treskový salát/Treska šalát

This is a classic Slovak recipe for cod cooked in a flavoured broth and then mixed with grated carrot, vinegar and mayonnaise. It makes an excellent refrigerator snack for the peckish, and a delicious quick bite for your lunch break. Fish recipes are not extensive in either country, but this salad is one of the most popular cod recipes.

1 Pour 3 litres/5¼ pints/12 cups cold water into a large pan. Add 250ml/8fl oz/1 cup white vinegar, the whole peppercorns and the bay leaves. Bring to the boil, and cook over medium heat for 5 minutes.

2 Add the cod fillets and cook for 13–15 minutes, or until just cooked and the fish flakes easily. Lift out the fish onto a plate and leave to cool.

3 Meanwhile, boil the carrots in the pan for 3–4 minutes, or until tender. Leave to cool and then grate using the fine side of a grater.

4 Use a fork to shred the cod into small pieces (about 1cm/½in). Combine the cod, carrots and onions together in a bowl. Add the rest of the white vinegar and the mayonnaise.

5 Season with salt and ground black pepper, then chill in the refrigerator for 1–2 hours before serving. Serve with fresh white rolls or rohlíky/rožky, or use the salad to fill sandwiches.

PER SERVING: Energy 334kcal/1392kj; Protein 38g; Carbohydrate 11g, of which sugars 9g; Fat 14g, of which saturates 2g; Cholesterol 104mg; Calcium 64mg; Fibre 2.4g; Sodium 310mg.

Chicken Pasta Salad
Těstovinový salát/Cestovinový šalát

This is a refreshing summer dish and, if you restrict the mayonnaise, makes a Czech version of a healthy light meal. Pasta is popular in both countries, and can be a useful, lighter alternative to traditional side dishes such as dumplings.

Serves 3–4

300–350g/11–12oz fusilli
500ml/17fl oz/2¼ cups boiling water
200g/7oz skinless chicken breast fillets
100g/3¾oz/scant 1 cup corn, frozen, fresh or canned
1 green (bell) pepper, diced
1 red (bell) pepper, diced
2 tomatoes, diced
200g/7oz Edam or Cheddar cheese, cut into 1cm/½in cubes
1 medium cucumber, diced
75g/3oz/⅓ cup mayonnaise
salt and ground black pepper

1 Cook the pasta according to the packet instructions. Pour 500ml/17fl oz/2¼ cups boiling water into another pan, add salt and boil the chicken breast fillets for 14–16 minutes. Check that they are completely cooked by cutting each breast in half. Remove the chicken from the water and leave to cool.

2 Drain and rinse the corn, if you are using canned. If using frozen or fresh corn, boil for 5 minutes, then leave to cool. Cut the chicken breast fillet into strips.

3 Combine the peppers, tomatoes, cheese and cucumber in a large bowl, and then stir in the mayonnaise and seasoning to taste. Chill the dish in the refrigerator before serving.

VARIATIONS
• Omit the chicken and serve the salad as a side dish to accompany barbecued meat.
• You can substitute tuna or ham for the chicken and add more vegetables such as onions and olives, if you like.
• Use feta cheese instead of Edam or Cheddar, and omit the mayonnaise if you prefer a lower-fat version.

PER SERVING: Energy 334kcal/2678kj; Protein 41g; Carbohydrate 72g, of which sugars 9g; Fat 23g, of which saturates 6g; Cholesterol 65mg; Calcium 49mg; Fibre 7.5g; Sodium 132mg.

Drowned Sausages

Utopenec

This delicious Czech snack is served in every pub.
The name actually translates as 'drowned man sausage'
after its inventor, a pub owner, met his end in this way.
You will need a large sterilized jar with a sealable lid that
holds 1.5 litres/2½ pints/6¼ cups liquid.

Serves 3–4

750ml/1¼ pints/3 cups boiling water
5ml/1 tsp ground black pepper
300ml/½ pint/1¼ cups white vinegar
15ml/1 tbsp sugar
15ml/1 tbsp whole black peppercorns
15ml/1 tbsp allspice
12 small Knockwurst sausages
2 white onions, peeled and sliced
  into rings
5–7 red chillies, or to taste, chopped
2 bay leaves
1–2 garlic cloves, peeled and chopped
salt
rye bread to serve

COOK'S TIPS

• Knockwurst sausages are available in German and Polish stores (the Czech term is vuřty).
• Make sure that the sausages and the glass jar that you are using aren't too cold and the mixture too hot when combining together, otherwise the jar might crack.

1 Put the boiling water into a large pan with a pinch of salt, the pepper, vinegar, sugar, peppercorns and allspice. Bring to the boil and simmer for 10 minutes.

2 Peel the skin off the sausages and cut lengthways through the middle, but leaving them attached, and put slices of onion in the centre of each sausage.

3 Place a layer of onions in the base of a sterilized jar. Add a layer of sausages, then cover them with onions and chillies. Continue this process until all the ingredients, including the bay leaves and garlic, are used.

4 Pour in the allspice liquid, covering all the ingredients. Cover and close the jar, tightening it as much as possible. Leave in a cool place for at least 5 days before eating. Serve chilled or at room temperature with rye bread.

PER SERVING: Energy 289kcal/1200kj; Protein 11g; Carbohydrate 18g, of which sugars 1g; Fat 26g, of which saturates 6g; Cholesterol 47mg; Calcium 105mg; Fibre 1.6g; Sodium 770mg.

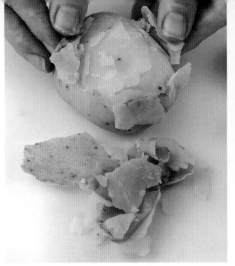

Vlassky Salad Snacks
Vlašský salát na chlebíčky

This salad is a traditional recipe used in both Republics. The word *vlašský* means 'walnut', which this salad doesn't contain, and to add to the confusion it is also sometimes called Italian salad or Welsh salad. The salad can be eaten on its own as a lunchtime snack, accompanied with a rohlíky or rožky and pivo (beer). As shown here, it is also a popular ingredient for chlebíčky – party finger food made with bread. These 'little breads' are made for special occasions, when guests visit, and always for Christmas and New Year. The salad is spread on sliced baguette or rohlíky with hard-boiled egg, tomatoes and gherkins.

Serves 4

500g/1¼lb potatoes, unpeeled
400g/14oz ham (processed)
300g/11oz can peas
30ml/2 tbsp of pickled gherkin juice
  (from the jar)
150g/5oz/generous ½ cup mayonnaise,
  or to taste
salt and ground black pepper

For the chlebíčky:
baguette slices
butter or garlic butter, for spreading
slices of ham
hard-boiled egg, sliced
gherkins, cut lengthways
pickled red pepper
tomato, sliced
grated Cheddar cheese (optional)

1 Cook the potatoes in boiling water for 25–30 minutes, or until soft. Leave to cool, then peel off the skins. Cut the potatoes and ham into thin strips.

2 Drain and rinse the canned peas under cold water. Mix the potatoes, ham and peas together in a bowl. Add salt, pepper and gherkin juice to taste.

3 Stir in the mayonnaise; you may wish to add more according to preference. Leave to chill in the refrigerator and serve chilled.

4 To make chlebíčky, evenly slice a French baguette (2cm/¾in thick), then butter each slice (you can add garlic butter, in which case add pressed garlic to the butter first).

5 Add the salad and top each baguette with a slice of ham, a slice of hard-boiled egg, a strip of gherkin, a strip of pickled red pepper, and a quarter of a slice of tomato, then, if preferred, sprinkle with finely grated Cheddar cheese.

VARIATIONS
• You can also add a finely diced onion to the salad. It helps to first cover the onion with boiling water for a few seconds before adding it, as this takes away the sharp flavour and makes it easier on the stomach.
• You can experiment by adding any or all of the following: Worcester sauce, Czech or Slovak 'full-fat' mustard, a few gherkins, a sour apple (popular in Slovakia), or white vinegar and sugar (dissolve the sugar in vinegar before adding to the salad).

PER SERVING OF VLASSKY SALAD: Energy 490kcal/2040kj; Protein 21g; Carbohydrate 27g, of which sugars 4g; Fat 34g, of which saturates 6g; Cholesterol 61mg; Calcium 68mg; Fibre 4.9g; Sodium 1926mg.

Serves 4

1kg/2¼lb pork fat
5ml/1 tsp salt
5ml/1 tsp ground black pepper
15–30ml/1–2 tbsp caraway seeds
    (optional)
rye bread, to serve

For the pâté

500g/1¼lb pork crackling
1 large onion, peeled and chopped
30ml/2 tbsp 'full-fat' Czech or Slovak
    mustard, or Polish mild mustard
1 garlic clove, peeled and crushed
    (optional)
salt and ground black pepper

Pork Crackling Pâté
Škvarky/Oškvarky

Pork crackling would usually be cooked in a pan rather than oven-roasted, and the economical dish then stored in the freezer for the winter months. It can be eaten as it is or made into this tasty pâté for serving with bread.

1 Dice the pork fat into 2cm/¾in cubes, then put into a large pan. Add 100ml/3½fl oz/scant ½ cup water and cook over low heat until golden. Stir occasionally to stop the fat sticking to the pan.

2 If you want the pork to be crispier, leave it to cook for a little longer. Use a coarse strainer to separate the fat from the crackling. Put the fat into a porcelain bowl and leave to cool. Keep it to serve on bread or to use for cooking and frying.

3 Using a dish towel or kitchen paper, squeeze the fat out of the crackling pieces. Spread the crackling out evenly on a baking tray, then add salt, pepper and caraway, if using, and leave to cool. Serve the crackling at room temperature with bread or make some into pâté.

4 To make the pâté, mince (grind) the crackling. Add the onion, mustard and garlic, if using, and season with salt and pepper, then mix well together. Serve the pâté cold on rye bread.

PER SERVING: Energy 376kcal/1559kj; Protein 24g; Carbohydrate 6g, of which sugars 4g; Fat 29g, of which saturates 10g; Cholesterol 66mg; Calcium 66mg; Fibre 0.9g; Sodium 567mg.

Serves 4

100ml/3½fl oz/scant ½ cup vegetable oil
1 onion, peeled and finely chopped
2 tomatoes, finely chopped
1 red (bell) pepper, finely chopped
1 egg, beaten
300g/11oz pork leg or pork fillet
   (tenderloin)
45ml/3 tbsp tomato purée (paste)
1–2 tsp chilli sauce or chilli powder
8 slices of Czech or Slovak rye bread
115g/4oz/1 cup grated Edam cheese
salt and ground black pepper
pickled vegetables, to serve

Fried Bread with Spicy Stir-fry

Topinky se směsí/Hrianky so změsou

The most traditional fried bread is spread with lots of garlic and enjoyed with a pint of beer. Here, it is served with pepper, tomatoes and egg, but it also works well as an accompaniment to soup.

1 Heat 15ml/1 tbsp oil in a pan and cook the onion for 5 minutes, or until softened. Add the tomatoes, pepper and egg, and stir quickly. Cook over gentle heat for 10 minutes.

2 Slice the pork into thin strips and put into a bowl. Add salt, pepper, 15ml/1 tbsp oil, add the tomato purée and the chilli sauce or chilli powder. Mix well.

3 Preheat 15ml/1 tbsp oil in a frying pan and fry the meat until brown. Add the tomato and pepper mixture, and fry for a further 10–15 minutes.

4 To make topinky or hrianky (fried bread) – preheat the remaining 55ml/3½ tbsp oil in a pan until hot and fry the bread until crisp. Spoon the stir-fry onto the fried bread and sprinkle with grated cheese. Serve with pickled vegetables.

PER SERVING: Energy 598kcal/2493kj; Protein 31g; Carbohydrate 30g, of which sugars 7g; Fat 40g, of which saturates 10g; Cholesterol 126mg; Calcium 297mg; Fibre 4.8g; Sodium 742mg.

Potato Dumplings with Pork Crackling
Škvarkové knedlíčky /Oškvarkové knedlíčky

These dumplings can be enjoyed on their own as a light meal, or used as a side dish for many main courses – whenever a recipe has a sauce then you can always add a dumpling! If you have some left over, fry them in a little butter the next day for a light snack.

Serves 3–4
750g/1lb 10oz potatoes, unpeeled
½ tsp salt
250g/9oz/2¼ cups plain (all-purpose) flour, plus extra for dusting
2 eggs, beaten
50g/2oz lard or white cooking fat, melted
15ml/1 tbsp oil

For the filling
1 onion, peeled and finely chopped
15ml/1 tbsp lard or white cooking fat
250g/9oz pork crackling cubes, or small pieces of smoked bacon
15ml/1 tbsp breadcrumbs

For the topping
100g/3¾oz smoked bacon, diced
30ml/2 tbsp lard or white cooking fat
2 white onions, peeled and finely chopped
200g/7oz pickled sauerkraut

COOK'S TIP
Potato dumplings are also commonly served plain. The method is the same, but don't make the filling in step 1, don't add the filling in step 4, and don't make the topping in step 5.

1 To make the filling, fry the onion in the lard or white cooking fat. Add the crackling and breadcrumbs, then cook for 5 minutes. Leave to cool.

2 To make the dumplings, boil the unpeeled potatoes for 15 minutes, or until they are just cooked. (You can do this step a day before and keep them in the refrigerator.) Peel the potatoes and grate them finely (a finer grind will make the dumplings softer).

3 Stir in salt, the flour, eggs and melted lard or white cooking fat. Work the dough into a solid consistency using your hands. The dumpling dough may feel more fluid than you are used to, but this ensures a light, fluffy consistency. On a work surface dusted with a little flour, roll the dough out until 1cm/½in thick and cut into roughly 5cm/2in squares.

4 Fill each square with 15ml/1 tbsp of the filling. Dip your hands into some flour, then form and roll the filling and dumpling dough into balls.

5 To make the topping, fry the bacon in 15ml/1 tbsp lard or white cooking fat, then add 1 onion and fry for 5 minutes or until golden. Drain the sauerkraut and squeeze out most of its juices, then add this to the onion and bacon. Cover with water, add salt, then cover and simmer for 15 minutes, or until soft.

6 Meanwhile, boil a large pan of water, add a pinch of salt and the oil. Drop in the dumplings and cook for 10–12 minutes, or until they have risen to the surface. Lift out with a slotted spoon and transfer to a warmed serving dish.

7 Fry the remaining onion in the remaining lard or white cooking fat for 5–10 minutes or until golden. Serve the dumplings with the fried onion on top, and the sauerkraut with bacon on the side.

PER SERVING: Energy 1038kcal/1335kj; Protein 48g; Carbohydrate 86g, of which sugars 9g; Fat 58g, of which saturates 19g; Cholesterol 225mg; Calcium 173mg; Fibre 6.5g; Sodium 1581mg.

FISH, MEAT & GAME

Carp and trout are widely found in the freshwater lakes of the Czech Republic and Slovakia and therefore also in both cuisines. The wholehearted emphasis in each country, however, is meat-based, with beef, pork, chicken, turkey, rabbit, goose, duck and game all having a central place on the menu. Along with meat products such as lard, the use of meat food sources derived from the need for hearty, protein-based foods. This supported the working population in previous centuries, providing them with the energy and resilience to combat the harsh winters. This dietary emphasis continues, although with some adaptations where fat content has been reduced with low-fat substitutes.

Freshwater delights & herby meats

While fish is not the main emphasis of the cuisine, carp and trout both feature consistently. Fish dishes are often baked, stuffed or fried, and Fried Carp and Potato Salad is a traditional favourite that is still served on Christmas Eve.

The meat dishes of both countries, particularly Slovakia, often have a humble simplicity because of the limited ingredients that would have been available. So a typical meal might have featured halušky dumplings (potato pasta) garnished with a little crispy bacon. Fridays were non-meat days, at which time a sheep's cheese dish or another sweet vegetarian option would have been served.

Many of the meat dishes in this chapter are familiar in both countries, albeit with subtle regional variations. Meat in Slovakia is more often breaded and fried in oil (schnitzel) or cooked and served in sauce. Hungarian influences can be seen in the Slovakian stews and goulashes, such as Szegediner Goulash.

Pork is used widely in both cuisines, and Roast Pork with Sauerkraut is seen as the Czech national dish. Streaky smoked bacon appears regularly and strips are often used to lace joints, giving additional flavour, fatty juices and tendernesss. Large joints and whole carcasses, such as chicken, turkey and rabbit, are served for big family meals, although rabbit is less often used now. Roasting such dishes in the oven or simmering them gently on the stove remains a straightforward way of creating nutritious meals.

Goose and duck provide simple roast dishes with a caraway and salt seasoning, and are often used as classic dishes for get-togethers and celebrations. Game, with its typical aromatic quality, is a delicacy during the autumn hunting season. It is usually served with rich and creamy sauces or as part of a stew.

Dumplings have always been a staple ingredient and main courses combine them with heavy, creamy sauces. The fluffy texture of the dumplings is perfect for absorbing the tantalizing flavours of the sauce.

Sauerkraut is an excellent accompaniment to heavy meat, and its sweet-sour taste acts as a neutralizer to the fat in both the meat and dumplings. Grilled sausages are also popular, served with mustard, horseradish and rye bread.

Fried Carp with Potato Salad

Smažený kapr s bramborovým salátem/
Vysmážaný kapor so zemiakovým šalátom

Carp fried in breadcrumbs and served with a potato salad is a traditional Christmas dish in both republics. Many years ago, the way to eat carp at Christmas was with a black sauce, but today fried carp is the most commonly prepared Christmas recipe. Potato salad is an excellent cold accompaniment and it also goes well with other fried dishes that the Czechs and Slovaks love to make, such as cheese, cauliflower, mushrooms and schnitzels.

Serves 4
100g/3¾oz/scant 1 cup plain
    (all-purpose) flour
2 eggs
30ml/2 tbsp milk
200–300g/7–11oz dried breadcrumbs
4 carp steaks
oil for shallow frying
1 lemon, cut into wedges, to garnish

For the potato salad
1kg/2¼lb old potatoes, unpeeled
250g/9oz carrots, peeled and left whole
200g/7oz/1¾ cups peas
150g/5oz gherkins, diced
3–4 tbsp brine from the gherkins
5–8 tbsp/75–120ml mayonnaise
salt and ground black pepper

COOK'S TIP
Make your own dry breadcrumbs from stale rohlíky/rožky. The author's grandmother would put them on the windowsill to dry out for a few days before breaking them up. You can also use breadcrumbs made from rye bread, but in this case the crumbs will be darker.

1 To make the potato salad, boil the unpeeled potatoes in salted water for 20–25 minutes, or until tender. Drain the water and leave the potatoes to cool for at least 30–45 minutes. (The longer the better, as you will have to peel them, and this is best done when cold.)

2 Meanwhile, boil the carrots whole in salted water for 10 minutes, or until tender. Cool, then cut into small pieces. Cook the peas in boiling salted water until tender. Drain and cool. Peel the skins off the cooled potatoes and dice into 1cm/½in pieces.

3 Gently combine the salad vegetables together, seasoning to taste with salt and ground black pepper. Add the brine, according to taste, and stir in mayonnaise. Chill until ready to serve.

4 Prepare three bowls: one with flour, one containing the eggs beaten with the milk, and a third with the breadcrumbs. Put these next to each other in the above order.

5 Sprinkle some salt over the fish, then dust each fillet in flour, dip into the egg and milk bowl, then coat thoroughly with breadcrumbs. Lastly, roll once more in the eggs and then the breadcrumbs, making sure to cover the whole fillet.

6 Pour enough oil into a frying pan to cover half the depth of the fillets. Preheat the oil and fry each fillet on both sides until golden, allowing 3–6 minutes per side – the oil should be at a high temperature for frying. Garnish each fillet with a wedge of lemon and serve with the potato salad.

PER SERVING: Energy 969kcal/4071kj; Protein 44g; Carbohydrate 14g, of which sugars 11g; Fat 41g, of which saturates 6g; Cholesterol 219mg; Calcium 253mg; Fibre 13.2g; Sodium 1076mg.

Serves 4

4 whole medium trout
4 tsp salt
60ml/4 tbsp caraway seeds
115g/4oz/½ cup butter
1 lemon, sliced, and tartar sauce (see
    page 96) to serve

For the new potatoes
800g/1¾lb new potatoes, unpeeled and
    left whole
3 garlic cloves, peeled and crushed
45ml/3 tbsp olive oil
salt
1 sprig fresh rosemary

Baked Trout with Caraway
Pstruh na kmíně /Pstruh s rascou

You won't find a huge selection of fish on a Czech or
Slovak menu, but any choices will be served fresh from
the local rivers. This is a classic recipe for trout, using
one of the favourite local flavourings, caraway seeds.

1 Preheat the oven to 180°C/350°F/
Gas 4. Cook the potatoes in salted
boiling water for 6 minutes. Drain and
cut the larger potatoes in half.

2 Mix the garlic with the olive oil and
pour over the potatoes. Shake the pan
to cover the potatoes with the oil, and
transfer to a roasting pan. Season with
salt and sprinkle over the rosemary.

3 Season each fish with 5ml/1 tsp salt
and 15ml/1 tbsp caraway seeds on the
inside and outside. Preheat the oven to
180°C/350°F/Gas 4.

4 Cut half the butter into slices and
spread it over an ovenproof dish that
will fit the trout. Add the fish and cover
with slices of the remaining butter.

5 Roast the potatoes on the top shelf
of the oven for 25 minutes, or until
golden and crispy, turning at least
once during cooking. Bake the fish on
the centre shelf for 30 minutes.

6 Serve the trout with a slice of lemon
and some tartar sauce for the potatoes.

PER SERVING: Energy 478kcal/2009kj; Protein 42g; Carbohydrate 36g of which sugars 2g; Fat 20g, of which saturates 2g; Cholesterol 0mg; Calcium 49mg; Fibre 2.4g; Sodium 622mg.

Serves 4

4 medium trout
50g/2oz/¼ cup butter
15ml/1 tbsp plain (all-purpose) flour
250ml/8fl oz/1 cup double (heavy) cream
100ml/3½fl oz/scant ½ cup white wine
pinch of freshly grated nutmeg
salt and ground black pepper
1 lemon, cut into wedges, and boiled new
   potatoes with parsley, to serve

Trout with Cream Sauce
Pstruh na smetaně/Pstruh so smotanou

This is a traditional recipe for pan-cooked trout. Many Czech and Slovak recipes include cream or a sauce – and frequently both. Here, the flavours of the cream, nutmeg and trout complement each other beautifully.

1 Season the fish inside and out with salt. Melt the butter in a frying pan and fry the trout for 5–8 minutes, turning, until golden.

2 Stir the flour into the cream and add this to the pan. Add the wine and nutmeg, and cook, covered, for 8–10 minutes or until cooked through.

3 Serve the trout with the sauce and a wedge of lemon, with boiled new potatoes sprinkled with parsley.

COOK'S TIP
Large sauce servings are typical – the amount of sauce here makes about a ladleful for each serving. Cut down the proportions if you feel this is too much.

PER SERVING: Energy 640kcal/2653kj; Protein 40g; Carbohydrate 4g, of which sugars 1g; Fat 51g, of which saturates 27g; Cholesterol 112mg; Calcium 56mg; Fibre 0.1g; Sodium 300mg.

Serves 4
750g/1lb 10oz potatoes, peeled and diced
25g/1oz/2 tbsp butter
2 egg yolks
1 egg, beaten
150g/5oz/2 cups dried breadcrumbs
4 large skinless chicken breast fillets
45ml/3 tbsp plus 200ml/7fl oz/scant
    1 cup vegetable or sunflower oil
8 slices ham (optional)
2 peaches in compôte (or 4 peach halves
    in compôte)
150g/5oz/1¼ cups of grated Edam
    cheese, or 8 slices of Edam
60ml/4 tbsp juice from the peach
    compôte
50ml/3½ tbsp double (heavy) cream
salt and ground black pepper
fresh salad, to serve

Peach Chicken & Croquettes

Kuřecí prsa s broskvou a sýrem/
Kuracie prsia s broskyňou a sýrom

This was one of my favourite restaurant foods when I was little. It is such a lovely combination of flavours, perfect for a family lunch. The recipe is popular in both countries and is unique to the two countries.

1 Cook the potatoes in salted boiling water for 15–20 minutes, until tender. Drain. Mash the potatoes with the butter and leave to cool. Stir the yolks into the mashed potato and roll into 2cm/¾in balls. Dip into the beaten egg and cover in breadcrumbs. Set aside. Preheat the oven to 200°C/400°F/Gas 6.

2 Pound the chicken breast fillets between two sheets of clear film (plastic wrap) with a rolling pin to tenderize them. Make the fillets quite thin, about 1cm/½in. Season.

3 Heat a pan with 45ml/3 tbsp oil and fry the chicken over medium heat for 5 minutes on each side. Transfer to a baking tray, setting aside the pan.

4 Top each breast with 2 slices of ham, if using. Add a peach half, top with grated cheese and bake for 5 minutes.

5 Heat the 200ml/7fl oz/scant 1 cup oil in a frying pan until hot (it should sizzle if you drop in a pinch of flour). Fry the croquettes for 5-10 minutes, or until they float and turn golden.

6 Using the chicken pan, add the compôte juice with the cream. Cook for 5 minutes, until the sauce thickens. Season. Serve the sauce on the chicken, with the croquettes and a fresh salad.

COOK'S TIP
The amount of sauce here makes a typically generous serving.

PER SERVING: Energy 919kcal/3845kj; Protein 52g; Carbohydrate 70g, of which sugars 11g; Fat 50g, of which saturates 17g; Cholesterol 303mg; Calcium 392mg; Fibre 5.6g; Sodium 914mg.

Red Pepper Chicken Paprikas
Kuře na paprice/Kurací paprikáš

Paprikáš is a Hungarian-influenced dish, eaten in Hungary since the early 19th century but adopted wholeheartedly in the Slovak Republic, also appearing occasionally in the Czech Republic.

1 Season the chicken pieces with salt. Plunge the tomato into boiling water for 30 seconds, then refresh in cold water. Peel away the skin, remove the seeds and dice the flesh. Set aside.

2 Heat the butter in a frying pan and fry the bacon and onion until brown. Take the pan off the heat and add the paprika.

3 Heat the oil in a different frying pan and brown the chicken fillets.

4 Add the fried bacon and onion, with the tomato, peppers and the stock. Mix well then cover the pan with a lid and cook over low heat for 35–40 minutes, or until tender.

5 Combine the cream with the flour in a small bowl, then add this to the pan and cook for a further 3–4 minutes.

6 Garnish with slices of pepper and a drizzle of sour cream. Serve with potato or bread dumplings.

Serves 4
4 skinless chicken breast fillets, or thighs
1 tomato
25g/1oz/2 tbsp butter
150g/5oz smoked bacon, diced
1 onion, peeled and chopped
25ml/1½ tbsp sweet or spicy paprika
45ml/3 tsp vegetable oil
2 red (bell) peppers, seeded and sliced
    into rings, plus extra to garnish
200ml/7fl oz/scant 1 cup chicken stock
400ml/14fl oz/1⅔ cups sour cream, plus
    extra to garnish
30ml/2 tbsp plain (all-purpose) flour
salt
potato dumplings (see pages 50–51) or
    bread dumplings (see page 13), to serve

PER SERVING: Energy 553kcal/2304kj; Protein 42g; Carbohydrate 21g, of which sugars 12g; Fat 34g, of which saturates 19g; Cholesterol 181mg; Calcium 14mg; Fibre 2.6g; Sodium 981mg.

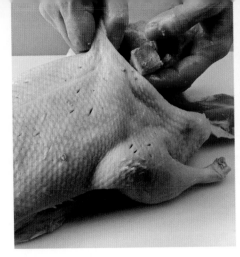  

Stuffed Roast Duck with Moravian Cabbage
Pečená kachna/Pečená kačka

Duck is a popular dish, but is also considered a delicacy. The traditional Czech and Slovak way of eating this bird is with cabbage and dumplings. There are many ways of preparing cabbage – this one, served with sweet-and-sour Moravian cabbage, is particularly tasty.

Serves 3–4

1 French baguette
100ml/3½fl oz/scant ½ cup milk
3 eggs
15ml/1 tbsp fresh chopped parsley
150g/5oz liver pâté
1 duck, about 2kg/4½lb, at room temperature
15ml/1 tbsp caraway seeds
salt and ground black pepper
dumplings (see pages 13 and 50–51) or potatoes, to serve

For the cabbage

1 pale green tightly packed cabbage, cut thinly
5ml/1 tsp caraway seeds
2 white onions, peeled and chopped
50g/2oz/¼ cup butter, or lard or white cooking fat
50g/2oz/½ cup plain (all-purpose) flour
1 potato, grated
15–30ml/1–2 tbsp caster (superfine) sugar
30–75ml/2–5 tbsp white vinegar

1 Preheat the oven to 190°C/375°F/Gas 5. Dice the baguette into 2.5cm (1in) cubes, then spread them out in a baking tray or ovenproof dish. Toast in the preheated oven for 10 minutes. Leave the oven turned on.

2 Beat together the milk, eggs, parsley and seasoning. Spread liver pâté over the bread cubes and pour the milk and egg over. Let the bread to soak up the liquid.

3 Prepare the duck by rinsing it under cold water inside and out, and drying it thoroughly with kitchen paper. Pierce the skin with a knife. Fill the body cavity with the soaked bread and pâté mixture and sew the opening closed. Season the outside with salt, pepper and caraway seeds and rub this mixture into the skin.

4 Put into a roasting pan and fill the base with 2cm/¾in of water. Roast for 2¼–3 hours, turning every 30 minutes and basting occasionally (cooking guidelines for duck is calculated as 30 minutes per 450g/1lb or until the internal temperature of the leg reaches 75°C/165°F). The duck is cooked when it is golden on the outside but the flesh is still slightly pink.

5 About 20 minutes before the duck is cooked, put the cabbage in a pan and add 5ml/1 tsp salt, the caraway seeds and a pinch of pepper. Add enough water to cover the cabbage, cover with a lid and bring to the boil. Simmer for 15 minutes, adding more water if necessary.

6 In a small pan, gently fry the onions in the butter or fat for 10 minutes, or until golden. Add the flour and cook for 2–3 minutes, stirring constantly. Add this to the cabbage with the grated potato. Add sugar and vinegar to taste – Moravian cabbage should be slightly sour. Adjust the seasoning, then cook for 10 minutes.

7 Leave the roasted duck to rest for 15 minutes before carving. Serve the duck, stuffing and cabbage with dumplings or boiled potatoes. Drizzle some of the fat from the roasting pan over the dumplings and meat.

PER SERVING: Energy 983kcal/4121kj; Protein 72g; Carbohydrate 73g, of which sugars 16g; Fat 47g, of which saturates 17g; Cholesterol 543mg; Calcium 282mg; Fibre 7.9g; Sodium 1279mg.

Roast Goose with Red Cabbage & Lokše

Nadívaná husa/Hus s plnkou

Goose is a favourite Christmas dish in both Republics and, because it is expensive, is only made for special occasions. It is delicious with Bohemian red cabbage and Slovak lokše, combining the tastes of both cultures in one meal.

Serves 4

1 goose, about 3kg/6lb/9oz
5ml/1 tsp salt
5ml/1 tsp ground black pepper
5ml/1 tsp caraway seeds

For the lokse

500g/1¼lb potatoes, unpeeled
2.5ml/½ tsp salt
150g/5oz/1¼ cups plain (all-purpose) flour, plus extra for dusting
115g/4oz/½ cup butter or goose fat, melted

For the red cabbage

1kg/2¼lb red cabbage, thinly sliced
1 onion, peeled and finely chopped
60ml/4 tbsp vegetable oil
30g/1¼oz/generous 2 tbsp caster (superfine) sugar
5ml/1 tsp caraway seeds
15ml/1 tbsp plain (all-purpose) flour
30ml/2 tbsp white vinegar
salt and ground black pepper

1 Preheat the oven to 190°C/375°F/Gas 5. Pour boiling water over the goose and pat dry with kitchen paper inside and out. Rub the salt and pepper over the skin and on the inside. Sprinkle the caraway seeds over the outside.

2 Pierce the skin, not the meat, all over. Put the goose in a roasting pan with the breast down and add 200ml/7fl oz/scant 1 cup water. Roast for 40 minutes, basting regularly. As it cooks, spoon or pour out most of the fat, and reserve.

3 Turn the goose over and roast for 2½ hours, basting regularly and removing the excess fat as before, until the goose is cooked, golden and crispy. Test by piercing the thickest part with the point of a knife or a skewer; the goose is ready when the juices run clear. Leave to rest, covered loosely with foil, for 30 minutes before serving.

4 While the goose is roasting, make the lokše. Cook the potatoes in their skins for 30 minutes, or until tender. Drain and leave to cool, then peel off the skins and mash the potatoes. Add the salt and flour, then work into a soft pliable dough. On a lightly floured surface, make into a long roll about 7.5cm/3in thick and cut into pieces about 5cm/2in thick. Roll each piece into a circle 1cm/1½in thick.

5 While the goose is resting, cook the lokse in a hot frying pan, without adding any oil, for 3-5 minutes on each side, or until golden. Spread each side of the cooked lokse with melted butter or goose fat, then serve warm.

6 About 30 minutes before the goose is ready to serve, make the red cabbage. Boil, covered, for 10 minutes, then drain and set aside. Fry the onion in the oil until brown, then add the cabbage, sugar, caraway seeds and a pinch of salt and pepper. Stir in the flour and 50ml/2fl oz/¼ cup water, and mix well.

7 Cover and simmer for 20 minutes. Stir in the vinegar and adjust the seasoning. Cook for 2–3 minutes. Serve the goose with the lokše and red cabbage.

PER SERVING: Energy 1468kcal/6119kj; Protein 83g; Carbohydrate 72g, of which sugars 20g; Fat 96g, of which saturates 17g; Cholesterol 61mg; Calcium 272mg; Fibre 11.6g; Sodium 1416mg.

Serves 4
4 pork fillets or tenderloins, about
    600g/1lb 6oz (roughly 150g/5oz each)
salt
200g/7oz/1¾ cups plain (all-purpose)
    flour
2 eggs, beaten
250g/9oz/3½ cups dried breadcrumbs
500ml/17fl oz/2¼ cups vegetable oil
lemon slices, to garnish
potato salad and a creamy cucumber
    salad, to serve

Schnitzel
Řízek/Rezeň

This is one of the most popular dishes across both countries – pork is the most common option but chicken and veal can also be used. The traditional accompaniment is a potato salad, an indispensable part of the cuisines.

1 Season the pork with salt and tenderize by putting it between two sheets of clear film (plastic wrap) and pounding it with a rolling pin into thin fillets.

2 Put the flour on a plate, the eggs in a shallow bowl and the breadcrumbs on another plate. Coat each fillet in flour, then dip in the eggs and coat in the breadcrumbs.

3 Heat the oil in a large frying pan until it is very hot and drop each loin steak in so that they are completely covered in oil.

4 Fry over high heat on both sides for 1 minute, then reduce the heat and cook for 5–6 minutes on each side, or until golden and cooked through. Garnish with a slice of lemon and serve with a potato salad and a cucumber salad made with cream.

VARIATION

To make stuffed schnitzels, place cheese and ham inside a fillet before coating, and fry for a little longer. Fold a flattened fillet over the filling, coat in breadcrumbs and put in the frying pan to seal the meat. You can also cut a pocket inside an unpounded fillet and stuff this.

PER SERVING: Energy 851kcal/3571kj; Protein 41g; Carbohydrate 87g, of which sugars 2g; Fat 40g, of which saturates 12g; Cholesterol 90mg; Calcium 166mg; Fibre 5.3g; Sodium 622mg.

Slovak Schnitzel
Černohorský Rezeň

This kind of schnitzel, wrapped in a flour and potato dough, comes from the western part of Slovakia near the mountains, hence its name Černohorský, which refers to this region.

Serves 4

4 large skinless chicken breast fillets (about 150g/5oz each)
2 potatoes, peeled and finely grated
2 eggs
15ml/1 tbsp dried marjoram
1 garlic clove, peeled and crushed
100ml/3½fl oz/scant ½ cup milk
about 115g/4oz/1 cup plain (all-purpose) flour, plus extra for dusting
100ml/3½fl oz/scant ½ cup vegetable oil
150g/5oz/1¼ cups grated cheese, such as Edam or Cheddar
salt and ground black pepper
chips (French fries) or fried potatoes, tartar sauce (see page 96) and salad, to serve

VARIATION
This recipe also works well with pork as a substitute for the chicken.

1 Tenderize the chicken by putting it between two sheets of clear film (plastic wrap) and pounding it with a rolling pin into thin fillets.

2 Mix the potatoes in a bowl with the eggs, marjoram, crushed garlic and a pinch of salt and pepper. Gradually add milk and enough flour to make a thick dough. Divide the dough into four pieces and roll or pat each out until large enough to wrap around a chicken fillet.

3 Dust each chicken fillet in flour and then wrap in potato dough.

4 Heat a frying pan with the oil over low-medium heat until just hot. Immediately, put the fillets into the pan and cook gently for 8-10 minutes on each side, or until the dough is golden and the chicken is cooked through.

5 Top the schnitzels with the grated cheese and serve warm. Serve with chips or fried potatoes, tartar sauce and a salad.

PER SERVING: Energy 595kcal/2496kj; Protein 55g; Carbohydrate 37g, of which sugars 2g; Fat 26g, of which saturates 26g; Cholesterol 251mg; Calcium 412mg; Fibre 2.2g; Sodium 622mg.

Serves 4
5ml/1 tsp caraway seeds
1kg/2¼lb pork joint
15g/½oz/1 tbsp lard or white cooking fat,
    or butter
1 onion, unpeeled and halved
2 garlic cloves, peeled and left whole
500ml/17fl oz/2¼ cups stock
pinch of salt and ground black pepper
dumplings (see pages 13 and 50–51) or
    boiled potatoes, to serve

For the sauerkraut
15ml/1 tbsp vegetable oil
1 onion, peeled and finely chopped
5ml/1 tsp plain (all-purpose) flour
600g/1lb 5oz sauerkraut, drained
    and washed
5ml/1 tsp caraway seeds
5ml/1 tsp caster (superfine) sugar,
    or to taste

Roast Pork with Sauerkraut
Vepřo, knedlo zelo/Bravčové mäso s kapustou a knedlíky

For many, this is the national Czech dish. It contains simple, hearty ingredients. Sauerkraut is often served with meat, and is particularly delicious with pork.

1 Rub salt, pepper and the caraway seeds into the pork. Heat the fat in a frying pan and brown the meat. Preheat the oven to 180°C/350°F/Gas 4.

2 Put the joint in a roasting pan, add the fat from the pan, the onion and garlic, then cover with 250ml/8fl oz/ 1 cup stock. Roast, covered in foil, for 1–1½ hours, or until tender, basting, and adding more stock if necessary.

3 Roast uncovered for 15–20 minutes to crisp the outside. Leave to rest for 5 minutes before carving.

4 To prepare the sauerkraut, heat the oil in a pan and cook the onion for 10 minutes. Stir in the flour, then add the sauerkraut. Add the caraway seeds, and season with salt and sugar.

5 Cover the pan with 1 litre/1¾ pints/ 4 cups water and cook, covered, for 30–40 minutes. The sauce should be thick.

6 Carve the pork and serve with boiled potatoes or dumplings and the sauerkraut, with the juices poured over.

PER SERVING: Energy 396kcal/1651kj; Protein 48g; Carbohydrate 10g, of which sugars 7g; Fat 18g, of which saturates 6g; Cholesterol 120mg; Calcium 115mg; Fibre 1.2g; Sodium 1468mg.

Serves 3–4

3–4 Anaheim chillies
1 onion, peeled and finely chopped
45ml/3 tbsp oil
500g/1¼lb minced (ground) pork
200g/7oz white rice, rinsed and drained
2 eggs, beaten
50g/2oz/1 cup dried breadcrumbs
30ml/2 tbsp plain (all-purpose) flour
5ml/1 tsp paprika
400g/14oz (2 tubes) tomato purée (paste)
45ml/3 tbsp caster (superfine) sugar
2 bay leaves
5ml/1 tsp dried marjoram
salt and ground black pepper
dumplings (see page 13 and pages
   14–15), boiled potatoes, rye bread or
   pasta, to serve
green salad, to serve

COOK'S TIP

Anaheim chillies are also known as
California green chillies. If you can't find
them, use long green (bell) peppers.

Stuffed Peppers
Plněná paprika

For this delightful summer dish, use sweet, pale-coloured
Anaheim chilli peppers if you can. They give the sauce
the right flavour and their fine skins allow the meat to
tenderize more quickly than other peppers.

1 Cut out the stalk and the seeds
from the whole chillies.

2 Fry the onion in 15ml/1 tbsp oil for
about 5–10 minutes, or until it is a
golden colour.

3 In a bowl, season the pork with salt
and pepper. Then add the onion, rice,
eggs and breadcrumbs.

4 Stuff the Anaheim chillies with the
meat mixture. Use the remaining
mixture to form round patties
3cm/1¼in in diameter.

5 In a large pan mix 30ml/2 tbsp oil
with the flour and cook over low heat
for 2–3 minutes, then add the paprika.

6 Add 1 litre/1¾ pints/4 cups cold
water and the tomato purée. Mix and
season to taste with salt and sugar.

7 Add the bay leaves and marjoram
and bring to the boil. Add the peppers
and meatballs, and cook over medium
heat for 35–40 minutes, or until the
peppers are tender. Serve the sauce
with dumplings, boiled potatoes, rye
bread or pasta, and a green salad.

PER SERVING: Energy 675kcal/2843kj; Protein 41g; Carbohydrate 86g, of which sugars 27g; Fat 21g, of which saturates 4g; Cholesterol 195mg; Calcium 101mg; Fibre 2.1g; Sodium 569mg.

Serves 4

500g/1¼lb sauerkraut, drained
30ml/2 tbsp vegetable oil
2 onions, peeled and finely chopped
600g/1lb 5oz pork shoulder, cut into
    2.5cm/1in cubes
10ml/2 tsp paprika
1 stock (bouillon) cube
30ml/2 tbsp plain (all-purpose) flour
250ml/8fl oz/1 cup double (heavy) cream
salt and ground black pepper
bread or potato dumplings (see page 13
    and pages 50–51), to serve

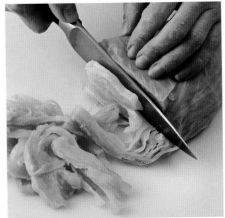

Szegediner Goulash
Segedínský guláš

This traditional Slovak dish, with a Hungarian influence, is very popular in pubs and restaurants. Generally it is served with bread dumplings, but it also combines well with potato dumplings or boiled potatoes.

1 Chop the sauerkraut into smaller pieces. Heat the oil in a pan and cook the onions gently for 10 minutes.

2 Add the pork and brown it. When the juices have started to release, season with salt, pepper and paprika (do not allow the paprika to burn).

3 Add the sauerkraut to the pan and add boiling water to cover. Crumble in the stock cube and mix well

4 Bring to the boil, then cover and simmer over medium heat, stirring occasionally, for 30 minutes or until the meat is tender.

5 When the meat is cooked, combine the flour and the cream in a small bowl and stir the mixture into the pan. Cook the contents for a further 5 minutes, then adjust the seasoning. Serve with bread or potato dumplings.

PER SERVING: Energy 777kcal/3217kj; Protein 32g; Carbohydrate 15g, of which sugars 7g; Fat 66g, of which saturates 30g; Cholesterol 188mg; Calcium136mg; Fibre 1.4g; Sodium 1247mg.

Serves 4

600g/1lb 5oz smoked pork loin
115g/4oz/½ cup butter
115g/4oz/1 cup plain (all-purpose) flour
250ml/8fl oz/1 cup double (heavy) cream
100g/3¾oz grated fresh horseradish
salt and ground black pepper
fresh chopped parsley, to garnish
bread dumplings (see page 13), to serve

Pork & Dumplings with Horseradish Sauce
Křenovka/Chrenová omáčka

Sauces have enormous prominence in both countries. So much so that the description of lunch might consist of just one word, the word for the sauce. Traditionally the meat would be interchangeable, but the sauce was indispensable to a good family sit-down meal. Here we have horseradish sauce, and this is a delicious recipe.

1 Put the pork in a large pan with 3 litres/5¼ pints/12 cups water and bring to the boil. Simmer over medium heat for 10 minutes, then drain and discard the water.

2 Cover the meat with 1.5 litres/ 2½ pints/6¼ cups boiling water. Cook for 2 hours, or until tender. Lift out the meat, then carve into portions and set aside. Reserve the stock and mix with 500ml/17fl oz/2¼ cups boiling water.

3 Heat the butter in a large pan, add the flour and cook for 2–3 minutes, stirring constantly. Gradually ladle in the pork stock, stirring constantly, to prevent lumps forming.

4 Combine the cream with the horseradish in a small bowl and add this to the sauce. Stir well and cook for 15 minutes. Season to taste, but be careful with the salt, as the cured meat is already quite salty. Garnish with parsley and serve with bread dumplings.

PER SERVING: Energy 1006kcal/4174kj; Protein 34g; Carbohydrate 26g, of which sugars 3g; Fat 86g, of which saturates 46g; Cholesterol 237mg; Calcium121mg; Fibre 2.9g; Sodium 273mg.

Serves 4

350g/12oz dried green peas, soaked overnight and drained, or 500g/1¼lb frozen peas
20g/¾oz/1½ tbsp butter
20g/¾oz/3 tbsp plain (all-purpose) flour
1.5 litres/2½ pints/6¼ cups milk
1 garlic clove, peeled and crushed
5ml/1 tsp dried marjoram
4 klobasa, or Hungarian sausages, or other suitable sausages
100ml/31/fl oz/scant ½ cup vegetable oil
salt
gherkins and fresh bread, to serve

VARIATIONS

• The pea sauce also goes well with a fried egg and it can be made into a vegetarian option by omitting the sausage.
• Use chickpeas instead of green peas.

Klobása & Thick Pea Sauce
Hrachová kaše/Hrachová kaša

This is often eaten as a hearty Saturday lunch. Like any pulse dish, the pea sauce is sustaining and healthy. In the Czech and Slovak Republics peas are usually bought dried, so they need to be soaked overnight.

1 Put the drained soaked peas into a pan with plenty of water to cover them well. Boil then simmer for 50–60 minutes, or until tender; salt the peas towards the end of the cooking time. If using frozen peas, cook in salted boiling water for 5–10 minutes or until tender. Drain.

2 Mash the peas coarsely. Heat the butter in a large pan, stir in the flour and cook for a few minutes. Add the milk, stirring constantly. Add the peas, garlic and marjoram, then add more salt to taste if necessary. Cook for a further 5 minutes.

3 Cut a few slits into the sausages, to make them open up nicely when frying. Heat the oil in a frying pan and cook the sausages over high heat until dark and crispy. Serve the pea sauce and sausages with gherkins and fresh bread.

COOK'S TIP

Large sauce servings are typical of Czech and Slovak dishes – the amount of sauce here makes a very generous serving.

PER SERVING: Energy 703kcal/2445kj; Protein 38g; Carbohydrate 26g, of which sugars 3g; Fat 86g, of which saturates 46g; Cholesterol 237mg; Calcium 121mg; Fibre 2.9g; Sodium 273mg.

Serves 4

1 kg/2¼lb floury potatoes, such as
   Russets, peeled and diced
salt
175g/6oz/generous 1½ cups plain
   (all-purpose) flour

For the savoury topping
40g/1½oz/3 tbsp butter
150g/5oz smoked bacon, diced
1 onion, peeled and chopped

For the sweet topping
60–90ml/4–6 tbsp icing (confectioners')
   sugar
60–90ml/4–6 tbsp poppy seeds, ground,
   or ground cinnamon
40g/2oz/3 tbsp butter, melted

COOK'S TIP
When shaping the potato mixture you can
add more water or flour, but don't overdo
the water and skimp on the flour.

Potato Škubánky
Škubánky/Džadky

In Slovakia this recipe is called džadky and is served with
fried onions and bacon, whereas in the Czech Republic it
is called škubánky, 'torn potato bits', and is served
sweet, with ground poppy seeds.

1 Cook the potatoes in salted boiling
water to cover for 20 minutes, or until
soft and easily broken apart. Drain off
half of the water, reserving it. Turn
down the heat leaving the potatoes
half-covered with water.

2 Mash the potatoes and gradually
add the flour at the same time (the
mixture should be firm, not runny –
add more potato water if necessary).

3 Cook for a further 2–3 minutes over
low heat and turn off the heat, leaving
the pan on the hob, and cover, then
leave the mixture steaming in the
warm pan for 15 minutes.

4 Using a tablespoon cut out little
even-sized balls and roll them into
oval shapes.

5 If you are using the savoury
topping, heat the butter in a frying
pan and fry the bacon until crispy,
then remove from the oil and set
aside. Fry the onion until golden.
Either add the onion and bacon to
the gnocchi separately or mix them
together first.

6 If you are using the sweet topping,
just top with icing sugar and ground
poppy seeds, then pour over some
butter just before serving.

PER SERVING: Energy 653kcal/2746kj; Protein 16g; Carbohydrate 100g, of which sugars 24g; Fat 24g, of which saturates 13g; Cholesterol 63mg; Calcium 89mg; Fibre 6.1g; Sodium 721mg.

Meatloaf with Tomato Sauce

Sekaná s rajskou omáčkou/Sekaná s paradajkovou omáčkou

You will always find a pork and beef meatloaf on a restaurant's menu, served with tomato sauce – the two marry perfectly. Serve either with plain dumplings or pasta.

Serves 4

15g/½oz/1 tbsp lard or white cooking fat, or butter
2 onions, peeled and finely chopped
700g/1lb 9oz/generous 3 cups minced (ground) pork
300g/11oz/1¼ cups minced (ground) beef
4–5 garlic cloves, peeled and crushed
2.5ml/½ tsp salt
pinch of ground black pepper
5ml/1 tsp dried marjoram
½ stock (bouillon) cube
2 eggs
100ml/3½/scant ½ cup milk
100–150g/3¾–5oz/2–2½ cups dried breadcrumbs
dumplings (see pages 13 or 14–15) or pasta, to serve

For the tomato sauce

30ml/2 tbsp vegetable oil
1 onion, peeled and chopped
30ml/2 tbsp plain (all-purpose) flour
350g/12oz passata (bottled strained tomatoes)
1.5 litres/2½ pints/6¼ cups stock
4 whole black peppercorns
2 allspice berries
1 bay leaf
15ml/1 tbsp caster (superfine) sugar,
5ml/1 tsp white vinegar, or to taste
salt

1 Preheat the oven to 180°C/350°F/Gas 4 and grease a baking tray. Heat the fat or butter in a pan and fry the onions for 5 minutes, or until softened. Put the minced meats into a large bowl and add the onions, garlic, salt, pepper and marjoram.

2 Dissolve the stock cube in 30ml/2 tbsp boiling water and add to the meat. Beat the eggs with the milk and gradually add this to the mince. Add 100g/3¾oz/2 cups breadcrumbs and mix together well using wet hands. Add more breadcrumbs if necessary so that you can form it into a compact loaf shape. Transfer to the baking tray.

3 Add water until it comes to about 5mm/¼in deep. Cover the baking tray with foil and roast for 1 hour, basting regularly, and adding more water if necessary. Remove the foil and roast for another 15–20 minutes to crisp the outside. Rest the meatloaf for 10 minutes before slicing.

4 While the meatloaf is roasting, make the tomato sauce. Heat the oil in a large pan, add the onion and cook gently for 5 minutes, or until softened. Add the flour and cook for 1 minute, stirring. Add the allspice, bay leaf and a little salt. Then stir in the passata and the stock, and cook for 20 minutes.

5 Sieve the sauce, then season to taste with salt, sugar and vinegar. Cook for another 2 minutes.

6 Allow the meatloaf to stand for 10 minutes before cutting. Serve the meatloaf with the tomato sauce and plain dumplings or pasta.

COOK'S TIPS

• Some people use rohlíky, rožky or soft white rolls in the meatloaf, which have first been soaked in water, then squeezed out, instead of adding milk to the eggs.
• Diced smoked bacon can be added to enrich the flavour.

PER SERVING: Energy 743kcal/3117kj; Protein 67g; Carbohydrate 51g, of which sugars 19g; Fat 31g, of which saturates 10g; Cholesterol 275mg; Calcium 165mg; Fibre 3.7g; Sodium 1403mg.

Roast Beef in Creamy Sauce
Svíčková/Svieckova

This dish is the epitome of Czech and Slovak cooking. Because of the marination process, it needs to be started preferably three days before serving the meal.

1 Cut slits into the joint and push the strips of bacon inside. Put the onion in a pan with the carrots, parsnip and celeriac and add 1.5 litres/2½ pints/6¼ cups water. Bring to the boil, add salt, vinegar, bay leaf, peppercorns and allspice, and cook for 5 minutes. Cool.

2 Put the meat into a large bowl, add the vegetables and stock so to cover most of the meat. Leave in the refrigerator for 2–3 days.

3 Dry the meat with kitchen paper. Heat the butter and brown the meat. Peel and chop the cooked onion, add to the pan, fry until golden and remove the joint. Drain the remaining vegetables and fry in the pan for 5 minutes. Remove the peppercorns and the allspice berry.

4 Cover the vegetables with 1 litre (34 fl oz) of marinating stock, add the meat, then cover and simmer for 1½ hours. Add more stock if needed.

5 Remove the meat and cut into 2.5cm/1in thick slices. Put the vegetables into a blender with two ladlefuls of stock and blend to a purée. Gradually add all the stock that was used to cook the meat until the sauce is smooth but not watery. Pour the sauce back into the pan.

6 Mix the flour with the cream and stir into the sauce. Simmer for 5 minutes. Add the sugar and vinegar. Return the meat to the sauce before serving. Garnish with a slice of lemon, and a teaspoon of cranberry jam. Serve with dumplings.

Serves 4

750g/1lb 10oz rump joint
80g/3¼oz smoked bacon, cut into thin strips
1 onion, left whole
4 carrots and 1 parsnip, peeled and chopped
1 parsnip, peeled and chopped
50g/2oz celeriac, peeled and chopped
100ml/3½fl oz/scant ½ cup white vinegar
1 bay leaf and 5 whole black peppercorns
1 allspice berry
50g/2oz/¼ cup butter
40g/1½oz/⅓ cup flour
250ml/8fl oz/1 cup double (heavy) cream
5–10ml/1–2 tsp caster (superfine) sugar
15ml/1 tbsp white vinegar, or to taste
salt
sliced lemon, cranberry jam and whipped cream, to garnish
potato or bread dumplings (see pages 13 and 50–51), to serve

COOK'S TIP
The amount of sauce makes about 3 ladlefuls per serving.

PER SERVING: Energy 881kcal/3654kj; Protein 46g; Carbohydrate 25g, of which sugars 14g; Fat 67g, of which saturates 37g; Cholesterol 235mg; Calcium105mg; Fibre 5.2g; Sodium 543mg.

Beef Goulash
Hovězí guláš/Maď'arský guláš

This is a recipe that men love to cook. It is also a popular pub dish, so much so that the pub's reputation will be closely linked to the success of the dish.

1 Season the beef with salt and pepper. Heat the fat or oil in a large pan over high heat and brown the meat. Remove the meat from the pan and set aside.

2 Fry the onions in the pan for 10 minutes, or until softened and golden; keep stirring to avoid them browning. Add the sweet and hot paprika to the onions, then fry for 2 minutes, being careful not to burn the paprika, which would turn bitter.

3 Cover with the stock, and add the meat, peppers, tomato purée and caraway seeds. Cover and simmer over low heat for 1½ hours, stirring occasionally, until the meat is tender.

4 When the meat is cooked, add the garlic and marjoram. Cook for a further 2–3 minutes and then adjust the seasoning. Garnish the dish with sliced onions and chillies, and serve with potato dumplings or bread dumplings.

Serves 4
700g/1lb 9oz casserole beef, cubed
40g/1½oz/3 tbsp lard or white cooking
    fat, or butter or oil
700g/1lb 9oz (about 6) white onions,
    peeled and finely chopped
10ml/2 tsp sweet paprika
5ml/1 tsp hot paprika
1.5 litres/2½ pints/6¼ cups beef stock
2 large red (bell) peppers, seeded and
    cut into thin strips
45ml/3 tbsp tomato purée (paste)
5ml/1 tsp caraway seeds
3–5 garlic cloves, peeled and crushed
15ml/1 tbsp dried marjoram
salt and ground black pepper
2 white onions, peeled and thinly sliced,
    and sliced red and green chillies
potato or bread dumplings (see pages 13
    or 50–51), to serve

PER SERVING: Energy 446kcal/1863kj; Protein 44g; Carbohydrate 29g, of which sugars 22g; Fat 18g, of which saturates 7g; Cholesterol 113mg; Calcium 86mg; Fibre 5.7g; Sodium 607mg.

Stuffed Cabbage Leaves
Plněná paprika/Plnená paprika

This delightful Slovak recipe is served in eastern Slovakia for special occasions, especially weddings. Because the dish takes a little while to prepare, be sure to make plenty, but even then you'll find it won't last long – because it is so good!

Serves 4

1 head tight-leaved, pale green cabbage
75ml/5 tbsp vegetable or sunflower oil
1 onion, peeled and finely chopped
5ml/1 tsp paprika
200g/7oz/1¾ cups cooked white rice (90g/3½oz/½ cup raw weight), rinsed and drained
100g/3¾oz sauerkraut, rinsed and drained
3 garlic cloves, peeled and crushed
300g/11oz/1¼ cups minced (ground) beef
100g/3¾oz/generous ½ cup diced smoked bacon
300g/11oz tomato purée (paste)
15ml/1 tbsp plain (all-purpose) flour
15ml/1 tbsp sugar and a drop of white vinegar, or to taste (optional)
salt and ground black pepper

1 Remove any discoloured outer leaves from the cabbage, and cut out the thickest part of the cabbage stem in the centre. Cook the whole cabbage in a large covered pan of salted boiling water. After 15–20 minutes, remove the leaves from the cabbage one by one as they become soft and peel away easily – you will have to do this in stages. You will need to peel about a half the cabbage. Set the leaves aside.

2 Cut out the thick central part of each leaf, and cut the largest leaves vertically in half.

3 Heat 45ml/3 tbsp oil in a small pan, add the onion and fry for 5 minutes, or until golden. Remove from the heat and stir in the paprika. In a large bowl, combine the onion and paprika, rice, sauerkraut, garlic, beef, bacon, 5ml/1 tsp salt and 5ml/1 tsp pepper and the remaining oil. Mix everything together well.

4 To stuff the cabbage leaves, put 30ml/2 tbsp of filling on to each cabbage leaf, starting at the top end, and roll up tightly into a cone with one side open and the other almost completely closed. Tuck in the open end. (You will not need to use all the leaves.)

5 Arrange the cabbage rolls in a large pan, squeezing them next to each other quite tightly; you can pile them on top of each other if necessary. Mix together the tomato purée with 500ml/17fl oz/2¼ cups water in small bowl, and pour this over the cabbage rolls to cover them. Add more water if necessary. Bring to the boil and simmer, covered, for 35 minutes.

6 Remove the cabbage rolls from the tomato sauce and keep them warm. Thicken the sauce with the flour, stirring the mixture and cooking for a further 5 minutes. Season to taste with salt and pepper (you can also add 15ml/1 tbsp sugar and a drop of white vinegar, if you like). Serve the cabbage rolls with the sauce.

PER SERVING: Energy 523kcal/2203kj; Protein 30g; Carbohydrate 69g, of which sugars 1g; Fat 16g, of which saturates 5g; Cholesterol 55mg; Calcium 103mg; Fibre 3.6g; Sodium 888mg.

Serves 4

1kg/2¼lb topside of beef
1 beef stock (bouillon) cube
dumplings (see pages 13 and 50–51) or
boiled potatoes, to serve

For the sauce

115g/4oz/½ cup butter
115g/4oz/1 cup plain (all-purpose) flour
200g/7oz fresh dill, finely chopped
250ml/8fl oz/1 cup sour cream
salt and ground black pepper

Beef with Dill Sauce

Hovězí maso s koprovou omáčkou/
Hovädzie mäso s kôprovou omáčkou

This recipe is a traditional one, served in both countries for Sunday lunch. I have eaten this classic combination of beef and dill sauce since I was little.

COOK'S TIP

The sauce here makes two ladlefuls per person. Cut down the proportions if you feel this is too much.

1 Put the beef joint in a large pan with 1.5 litres/2½ pints/6¼ cups water and crumble in the stock cube. Cook for 1 hour, or until tender. Remove from the broth and cut into 1cm/½in slices.

2 To make the sauce, melt the butter in another large pan, and add the flour. Cook for 3 minutes, stirring. Gradually ladle the beef broth into the flour mixture, stirring constantly to avoid lumps from forming.

3 Combine the dill with the sour cream in a small bowl and add to the sauce. Cook for a further 3 minutes. Season to taste with salt and pepper.

4 Add the slices of beef to the sauce, then serve with dumplings or boiled potatoes.

VARIATION

For a vegetarian option make the dill sauce with a vegetable stock (bouillon) cube rather than beef broth, and serve with boiled potatoes and a hard-boiled egg.

PER SERVING: Energy 756kcal/3151kj; Protein 61g; Carbohydrate 25g, of which sugars 3g; Fat 46g, of which saturates 27g; Cholesterol 231mg; Calcium 286mg; Fibre 1.0g; Sodium 660mg.

Serves 4

4 fillets of beef rump (round) steak
60ml/4 tbsp Czech/Slovak 'full-fat'
   mustard or mild polish yellow mustard
100g/3¾oz rindless rashers (strips)
   smoked bacon
2 hard-boiled eggs, halved top to bottom
4 gherkins
30ml/2 tbsp vegetable oil
50g/2oz/½ cup plain (all-purpose) flour
250ml/8fl oz/1 cup double (heavy) cream
salt and ground black pepper
rice or dumplings, to serve

Spanish Birds
Španělští ptáčci/Hovädzia roláda

This dish is a classic in both countries. 'Spanish birds' is a literal translation, and the expression probably comes from a similar Spanish meat-roulade dish.

1 Tenderize the steaks by putting them between two sheets of clear film (plastic wrap) and pounding them with a rolling pin until about 1cm/½in. Season with salt and pepper.

2 Spread one side of each fillet with 15ml/1 tbsp mustard. Put a quarter of the bacon, half an egg and a gherkin on top of the mustard, in the centre of the fillet.

3 Roll the meat fillet around the filling, into a roulade, and secure in place with cocktail sticks (toothpicks) or metal skewers, or alternatively tie it with thread.

4 Heat the oil in a pan and fry each roulade over high heat, turning, until the meat releases its juices and browns. Add 200ml/7fl oz/scant 1 cup water, cover and simmer for 25–30 minutes, or until tender.

5 Remove the roulades from the pan, leaving the sauce. Remove the cocktail sticks, skewers or thread. Combine the flour with the cream and add to the cooking juices. Season with salt and pepper and cook for 3 minutes.

6 Return the roulades to the pan to heat them through. Serve the roulades and sauce with rice or dumplings.

PER SERVING: Energy 780kcal/3241kj; Protein 51; Carbohydrate 12g, of which sugars 3g; Fat 59g, of which saturates 30g; Cholesterol 565mg; Calcium 123mg; Fibre 0.5g; Sodium 1196mg.

Lamb with Creamy Spinach
Pečené jehněčí maso/Pečené jahňacie mäso

Spinach is a frequent accompaniment to sweet-flavoured lamb, which is traditionally cooked at Easter and other special occasions. This recipe uses herbs and the optional addition of stinging nettles, an easy-to-gather ingredient that sometimes appears in Czech and Slovak stuffings, salads, meat roasts and tea infusions.

Serves 4

5ml/1 tsp fresh chopped chives
5ml/1 tsp chopped stinging nettle leaves (optional)
10ml/2 tsp ground coriander
2 garlic cloves, peeled and chopped
1 tsp salt
1 tsp ground black pepper
20g/¾oz/1½ tbsp butter, softened
600g/1lb 5oz boned leg of lamb
1 spring onion (scallion), chopped
400ml/14fl oz/1⅔ cups stock
5ml/1 tsp plain (all-purpose) flour
potato dumplings (see pages 50–51) or boiled potatoes, to serve

For the creamy spinach

15g/½oz/1 tbsp butter
60ml/4 tbsp vegetable oil
1 onion, peeled and finely chopped
500g/1¼lb frozen chopped spinach
500ml/17fl oz/2¼ cups stock
30ml/2 tbsp plain (all-purpose) flour
20ml/4 tsp milk
5 garlic cloves, peeled and crushed
200ml/7fl oz/scant 1 cup double (heavy) cream
salt and ground black pepper

1 Preheat the oven to 230°C/450°F/Gas 8. Mix together the chives, stinging nettles, if using, coriander, garlic, salt, pepper and butter. Rub this seasoned butter all over the lamb, put into a roasting pan, cover with foil and leave to rest for 1 hour.

2 Add the spring onion to the pan and pour in the stock to come to about 2cm/¾in up the sides of the roasting pan. Roast for 20 minutes, then reduce the oven temperature to 180°C/350°F/Gas 4 and roast for 45 minutes, or until cooked to your liking, basting regularly and topping up with water if necessary.

3 Remove the roast from the oven, cover with foil and leave to rest for 15 minutes before carving.

4 When the lamb is 15 minutes towards the end of cooking, make the creamy spinach. Heat the butter and 30ml/2 tbsp oil in a pan, add the onion and fry for 3–4 minutes, or until golden. Add the frozen spinach, and stock, cover and simmer over low heat for 10 minutes, or until all the spinach has defrosted.

5 Heat the remaining oil in a pan and add the flour. Cook, stirring, for 2–3 minutes, then stir in the milk. Gradually stir this into the spinach, and cook for 10-15 minutes. Add the garlic, cream and seasoning to taste. Cook for a further 2 minutes. Keep warm.

6 While the meat is resting, make a gravy. Strain the cooking juices from the roasting pan into a small pan and stir in the 5ml/1 tsp flour. Cook for 3 minutes, stirring. Serve the Lamb with Creamy Spinach with potato dumplings or boiled potatoes.

PER SERVING: Energy 693kcal/2873kj; Protein 37g; Carbohydrate 11g, of which sugars 4g; Fat 56g, of which saturates 30g; Cholesterol 215mg; Calcium 278mg; Fibre 5.2g; Sodium 1210mg.

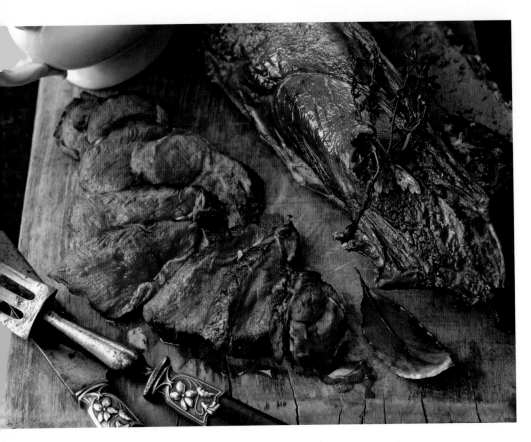

Serves 4
700g/1lb 9oz venison loin or whole fillet
50ml/2fl oz/¼ cup vegetable oil
15ml/1 tbsp plain (all-purpose) flour
salt and ground black pepper
cranberry jam, to garnish
boiled, sautéed or creamed potatoes,
    to serve

For the marinade
500ml/17fl oz/2¼ cups red wine
4 juniper berries
1 carrot, peeled and chopped
1 garlic clove, peeled and left whole
1 onion, peeled and quartered
1 bay leaf
1 thyme sprig, 1 rosemary sprig and
    1 parsley sprig
15ml/1 tbsp vegetable or sunflower oil
2.5ml/½ tsp ground black pepper

Saddle of Venison
Srnčí hřbet/Srnčí chrbát

Deer is a popular game meat during the hunting season.
The red wine marinade is a classic accompaniment – and
the serving quantity is typically generous.

1 Combine all the marinade ingredients
in a large bowl and add the venison.
Leave to marinate in the refrigerator for
24 hours, turning over after 12 hours.
Lift out from the liquid and pat dry with
kitchen paper. Reserve the marinade.

2 Preheat the oven to 200°C/400°F/
Gas 6. Heat the oil in a frying pan and
sear the venison for 2–3 minutes per
side until brown. Remove the meat
from the oil, put in a roasting pan
and add 50ml/2fl oz/¼ cup of the
marinade liquid and the vegetables.

3 Roast, covered with foil, for around
30 minutes, or until medium rare.

4 Remove the venison from the pan
and leave to rest for 10 minutes, when
it will continue to cook. Carve into
5cm/2in thick slices and keep warm.

5 Strain the sauce from the vegetables
into a pan, and strain in the remaining
marinade. Simmer for 15 minutes, or
until the sauce has reduced. Add the
flour and cook for 3 minutes. Season
with salt and ground black pepper.

6 Put the venison in the sauce, if not
serving immediately. Garnish the
venison with cranberry jam and serve
with boiled, sautéed or creamed
potatoes, drizzled with the wine sauce.

PER SERVING: Energy 339kcal/1420kj; Protein 39g; Carbohydrate 3g, of which sugars 0g; Fat 20g, of which saturates 3g; Cholesterol 88mg; Calcium 14mg; Fibre 0.1g; Sodium 195mg.

Rabbit with Mushroom Sauce
Králík na houbách/Králík na šampiónoch

Many Czech and Slovak households would breed rabbits for eating. This is less common nowadays, but the meat remains popular. It is very lean, with a similar consistency and taste to chicken, except darker.

Serves 4

150g/5oz/10 tbsp butter
1 large rabbit, at least 700g/1lb 9oz, cut into 4 portions (two rib sections and two back sections)
60g/2½oz carrots, unpeeled and chopped
50g/2oz parsnips, unpeeled and chopped
1 onion, unpeeled and chopped
200g/7oz sliced button (white) mushrooms
30ml/2 tbsp flour
200ml/7fl oz/scant 1 cup double (heavy) cream
salt and ground black pepper
bread dumplings (see page 13), boiled potatoes or pasta, to serve

COOK'S TIP
The amount of sauce here makes about 2 ladlefuls for each serving. Cut down the proportions if you feel this is too much.

1 Heat 25g/1oz /2 tbsp butter in a pan and brown the rabbit on both sides for 2–3 minutes over high heat. Put the carrots, parsnips, onion and the rabbit into a large pan. Cover with boiling water, add salt and cook, covered, over low heat for 1–1½ hours, or until tender.

2 Lift out the meat and set aside, drain the vegetables and reserve the stock. Purée the vegetables in a blender, then gradually ladle the stock into the blender to make a thick sauce (do not use all the stock, if the sauce becomes too thin). Season to taste.

3 Heat 50g/2oz/¼ cup butter in a pan and add the mushrooms. Cook, covered, for 10–15 minutes, or until golden and soft. Remove the mushrooms from the butter and set aside.

4 Heat the remaining butter in another large pan, add the flour and cook for 2–3 minutes. Add the vegetable sauce, the mushrooms and the rabbit portions. Stir in the cream and cook for a further 4 minutes. Serve with bread dumplings, boiled potatoes or pasta.

PER SERVING: Energy 735kcal/3044kj; Protein 31g; Carbohydrate 14g, of which sugars 6g; Fat 62g, of which saturates 38g; Cholesterol 253mg; Calcium 115mg; Fibre 1.5g; Sodium 408mg.

Potato Pasta

Haluŝky

This is the national dish of Slovakia. Similar to Italian gnocchi, it is simple, home-cooked food at its best. If you want an authentic dish, you need to use bryndza, a sheep's cheese from Slovakia, to top the haluŝky. If you can't get hold of this, however, it is fine to use other types of soft cheese and sheep's cheese. This dish is usually served with a glass of milk or kefír.

Serves 4

600g/1lb 5oz potatoes, peeled and grated
5ml/1 tsp salt
about 185g/6½oz/1⅔ cups plain
   (all-purpose) flour, and extra for dusting
1 egg, beaten
300g/11oz smoked bacon from a block,
   diced (the Slovaks use oravská slanina
   bacon from the Orava region)
15ml/1 tbsp vegetable oil
250g/9oz/generous 1 cup bryndza, or feta
   or cottage cheese
200ml/7fl oz/scant 1 cup double (heavy)
   cream

1 In a bowl, combine the potatoes with the salt, flour and egg to make a thick, sticky dough; if the dough is too runny (if it doesn't stick to the wooden spoon) add more flour, a tablespoonful at a time.

2 Bring a large pan of water to the boil. Put the bacon cubes in a pan with the oil over a low heat, keeping an eye on them until they are crispy.

3 When the water is boiling, and using a haluŝky strainer (haluskár), drop the dough into the boiling water. Alternatively, (this is the original way) transfer the dough to a chopping board that you have lightly dusted with flour and, using a sharp knife, cut little pieces, roughly 2cm/¾in long and 1cm/½in thick but the smaller the better, and drop them into the boiling water as you cut them.

4 The haluŝky will drop to the bottom of the pan. Give them a gentle stir. They are ready when they change colour and float to the top of the water, after about 7–10 minutes. Scoop them out with a slotted spoon or sieve as they cook. They will cook at different times because of their uneven shapes and the fact that they have been added to the water in stages. Leave to drain for 2 minutes.

5 Put the haluŝky into a bowl, mash the bryndza and double cream into a sauce, and then mix the sauce with the haluŝky. Serve with the cooked bacon scattered over each portion.

COOK'S TIPS

• The traditional recipe for haluŝky does not include an egg, but it is added here because it helps to bind the dough together.
• The other way of serving haluŝky is with sauerkraut and bacon, in which case fry 200g/7oz diced bacon, then add 400g/14oz sauerkraut before mixing with the haluŝky.
• You can also try using a potato ricer instead of a haluŝky strainer, this will give you smaller lumps of dough, which will cook faster.

PER SERVING: Energy 892kcal/3716kj; Protein 32g; Carbohydrate 64g, of which sugars 3g; Fat 58g, of which saturates 31g; Cholesterol 210mg; Calcium 335mg; Fibre 4.1g; Sodium 2590mg.

SWEET MAINS
& VEGETARIAN
DISHES

Sweet main courses form a significant part of the Czech and Slovak diets. This genre of main meal was introduced to give more options for non-meat Fridays, a day of atonement for orthodox Catholics. Because both cuisines are so meat-orientated, few follow a strictly vegetarian diet. But many still avoid meat on Fridays when thick soups and light vegetarian meals, such as fried cheese, might be on offer. So, here sweet mains and savoury vegetarian options form a natural pairing.

Root vegetables, cheese & sweet meals

Vegetarians are rare in Slovakia and the Czech Republic as people are fond of their diet of red meat and other animal products. However, the Catholic population, mostly based in Slovakia but also in many areas of the Czech Republic, still avoid meat on Fridays, a custom that was first introduced as a religious penance.

Vegetables also form a good basis of economical meals for families on a low budget, so there are various authentic vegetarian dishes to try out, among them Potato Goulash, Halušky with Sauerkraut, the ever-present sauerkraut variations or Lečo, a sweet pepper stew. For economy's sake, many dishes include flour, such as Langoš which is made from bread dough leftovers. Another budget classic includes a type of ravioli called pirohy, typically served with sheep's cheese, cottage cheese, or for a sweet option, jam or ground walnuts with melted butter and sugar.

A unique characteristic of both cuisines is the use of sweet dishes as a main course. This tradition also stems from meatless Fridays when the substantial lunchtime meal would often consist of a thick vegetable soup with a sweet main course and no dessert. Examples here include Sweet Semolina Pudding and Baked Rice Pudding, the latter prepared with fruit, egg yolks and whisked egg, and this is always a popular choice for children. Another delight are the deliciously fluffy Fruit Dumplings prepared with the thick-textured local plum jam or whole fruit such as plums, strawberries, cherries, apricots, bilberries and peaches, coated in dough, steamed or boiled, and served with the sweet additions of sugar, cream and milled poppy seeds. Fruit such as apples and plums is also offered as a side dish to the main meal of the day in Slovakia.

Vegetarian savouries are often adapted from meat dishes, perhaps replacing meat content with a hard-boiled egg, vegetable or bean ingredient. In fact, a number of the dishes from the fish, meat and game chapter have vegetarian alternatives. Also, while there is an established culture of meat in this part of the world, there have been noticeable shifts towards a more vegetarian emphasis.

Sweet Pepper Stew
Lečo

Lečo, popular in both countries, is the base for many sauces. It can also be enjoyed as a light dinner with a slice of rye bread. Experiment with the recipe by adding your favourite vegetables and a couple of eggs.

Serves 6–8
5 green peppers
30ml/2 tbsp vegetable oil or melted lard
1 onion, sliced
450g/1lb plum tomatoes, peeled and chopped
15ml/1 tbsp paprika
sugar and salt, to taste
grilled bacon strips, to garnish
crusty bread, to serve

1 Wipe the green peppers, remove the cores and seeds and slice the flesh into strips.

2 Heat the oil or lard. Add the onion and cook over a low heat for 5 minutes until just softened.

3 Add the strips of pepper and cook gently for 10 minutes.

4 Add the chopped tomatoes and paprika and season to taste with a little sugar and salt.

5 Simmer the mixture over a low heat for 20–25 minutes. Serve immediately, topped with the strips of grilled bacon and accompanied by crusty bread.

VARIATION
To vary this recipe, add 115g/4oz/1 cup sliced salami or some lightly scrambled eggs to the vegetables.

PER SERVING: Energy 118kcal/492kJ; Protein 3.2g; Carbohydrate 18.4g, of which sugars 16g; Fat 4g, of which saturates 0.6g; Cholesterol 0mg; Calcium 35mg; Fibre 4.3g; Sodium 15mg.

Baked Potatoes with Cream
Zapečené brambory/Zapékané zemiaky

This recipe is reminiscent of the French dauphinois potatoes, although much simpler and suitable for a vegetarian main course, rather than just a side dish. The cream content makes this a rich and filling dish.

Serves 3–4

500g/1¼lb floury potatoes, unpeeled
50ml/2fl oz/¼ cup olive oil
2 red (bell) peppers, seeded and cut into thin strips
1 red onion, peeled and thinly sliced
1 courgette (zucchini), diced
150g/5oz canned corn
250ml/8fl oz/1 cup double (heavy) cream
1 egg
115–150g/4–5oz/about 1 cup grated Cheddar or Edam cheese
5ml/1 tsp paprika
salt and ground black pepper
fresh green salad, to serve

VARIATION

You can substitute different vegetables, or use a selection of the vegetables and use the gratin as a side dish.

1 Boil the potatoes in their skins for 10 minutes, or until they are almost completely cooked but still firm in the middle. Drain and leave to cool. Preheat the oven to 190°C/375°F/ Gas 5.

2 Heat the olive oil in a frying pan, add the peppers, onion, courgette and corn, and fry for 5 minutes. Season with salt and pepper.

3 Pour the cream and egg into a small bowl and whisk until mixed. Add this to the vegetables and remove from the heat.

4 Peel the potatoes and cut into small pieces. Mix with the vegetables and transfer to a baking tray. Top with grated cheese, if you are using. Sprinkle with paprika and bake for 20–25 minutes or until golden. Serve with a fresh green salad.

PER SERVING: Energy 2607kcal/10808kj; Protein 65g; Carbohydrate 132g, of which sugars 4g; Fat 205g, of which saturates 116g; Cholesterol 701mg; Calcium 1269mg; Fibre 17.9g; Sodium 1532mg.

Serves 4

15ml/1 tbsp oil

2 white onions, peeled and finely chopped

1kg/2¼lb waxy potatoes, peeled and cut into cubes

15ml/1 tbsp red paprika seasoning

5–10ml/1–2 tsp caraway seeds

1.5 litres/2½ pints/6¼ cups of boiling water

2 vegetarian stock (bouillon) cubes (preferably beef flavour vegetarian stock)

2 garlic cloves, peeled and crushed

120ml/4fl oz/½ cup double (heavy) cream

30ml/2 tbsp plain (all-purpose) flour

5ml/1 tsp dried marjoram

salt

rye bread, to serve

Vegetarian Potato Goulash
Bramborový guláš/Zemiakový guláš

Although goulash is usually made with meat, this is a tasty vegetarian option with lots of flavour. You might find this combination of potatoes and bread quite unusual, but it is a popular, warming meal.

1 Heat the oil in a large pan and fry the onions for 5–10 minutes, or until golden. Add the potatoes, paprika and caraway seeds.

2 Add the boiling water, the stock cubes and garlic. Bring to the boil, then cover and cook over medium heat for 25–30 minutes, or until the potatoes are soft.

3 In a separate bowl mix the cream with the flour. Add this to the goulash and cook for a further 3 minutes. Add marjoram and salt to taste. Serve with rye bread.

VARIATIONS

• You can add other vegetables, such as green (bell) peppers or button mushrooms to the goulash.

• For a non-vegetarian option, you can make the goulash with chopped frankfurter sausages.

PER SERVING: Energy 427kcal/1787kj; Protein 7g; Carbohydrate 54g, of which sugars 8g; Fat 22g, of which saturates 11g; Cholesterol 41mg; Calcium 65mg; Fibre 4.6g; Sodium 724mg.

Serves 4

200g/7oz tagliatelle

65g/2½oz/5 tbsp butter

50g/2oz roasted flaked (sliced) almond

185g/6½oz/1⅓ cups ground poppy seeds

5ml/1 tsp cinnamon

15–30ml/1–2 tbsp vanilla sugar

150g/5oz/generous ⅔ cup Tvaroh sweet cheese, or quark or cottage cheese mixed with 45ml/3 tbsp of icing (confectioners') sugar

icing (confectioners') sugar for dusting

salt

Pasta with Poppy Seeds
Nudle s mákem/Cestoviny s mákom

This is a simple Czech recipe that I remember eating frequently in my childhood. Most Czech and Slovak households have a manual pasta maker and if you have one you might like to make your own.

1 Cook the pasta in salted boiling water for 4–6 minutes or according to the packet instructions. Drain.

2 Meanwhile, melt the butter in a pan, add the almonds, ground poppy seeds, cinnamon and vanilla sugar, and cook, covered, over low heat for 2–3 minutes.

3 Serve the noodles hot, topped with Tvaroh cheese, or the soft cheese mixture, and the poppy seeds and almonds, and dust with icing (confectioners') sugar.

VARIATION

Another favourite topping is made with melted butter, icing sugar and cocoa.

PER SERVING: Energy 733kcal3066kj; Protein 23g; Carbohydrate 66g, of which sugars 22g; Fat 43g, of which saturates 11g; Cholesterol 35mg; Calcium141mg; Fibre 5.5g; Sodium 125mg.

Serves 4

400g/14oz Edam cheese, or cauliflower
   florets or button (white) mushrooms
2 eggs
30ml/2 tbsp milk
pinch of salt
115g/4oz/1 cup plain (all-purpose) flour
300g/11oz/4⅕ cups dried breadcrumbs
200ml/7fl oz/scant 1 cup vegetable oil
cucumber, tomato and onion salad, to serve

For the tartar sauce
45ml/3 tbsp mayonnaise
1 small onion, peeled and diced into
   small pieces
1 gherkin, finely grated

For the chips (fries)
500–600g/1¼–1lb 5oz floury potatoes,
   peeled and cut into chips
30ml/2 tbsp vegetable oil
salt and ground black pepper

Three Fried Dishes and Chips

Smažený sýr, květák a žampio'ny/ Vysmázaný sýr, karfiol a sămpio'ny

These three types of fried dishes, with cheese, mushrooms
and cauliflower, are found on most restaurant menus in
both Republics. They are delicious served with tartar sauce.

1 Preheat the oven to 200°C/400°F/
Gas 6. Make the tartar sauce by
mixing the mayonnaise with the
onion and gherkin. Transfer to a
serving bowl and chill.

2 Put the cut chips into cold water for
5 minutes. Drain, dry thoroughly and
put into a dry bowl. Pour over the oil
and season, then shake the bowl to
coat evenly with oil. Tip on to a baking
sheet and bake for 40–45 minutes, or
until golden, turning once.

3 If you are using cheese for frying,
cut it into four equal parts. If using
cauliflower, parboil it for 2–3 minutes.

4 Beat the eggs with the milk and
salt. Put the flour and breadcrumbs
on separate plates. Coat each piece
of cheese, cauliflower or mushroom
in flour, then dip into the egg mixture
and coat in the breadcrumbs; repeat
the last two stages three times to
make sure none of the cheese or
vegetable is showing.

5 When the chips are almost ready,
preheat the oil in a frying pan and fry
each breadcrumb-coated piece of
food for 4–6 minutes on each side,
or until golden. Serve warm with
the chips and tartar sauce, with a
cucumber, tomato and onion salad.

PER AVERAGE SERVING: Energy 827kcal/3475kj; Protein 30g; Carbohydrate 109g, of which sugars 7g; Fat 33g, of which saturates 9g; Cholesterol 149mg; Calcium 456mg; Fibre 9.4g; Sodium 1211mg.

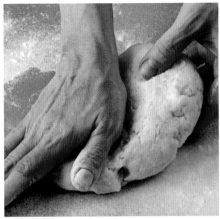

Slovak Cheese Pie
Pagáče

This is a savoury Slovak recipe, excellent as a little snack or as a light lunch. There are two other kinds of pagace filling: pork crackling and potato.

1 Sift the flour with the baking powder into a bowl. Add the sour cream, salt, butter and grated cheese.

2 Stir together the ingredients, then gently knead the dough, adding more flour if you find that the mixture is too sticky. Wrap in clear film (plastic wrap) and chill in the refrigerator for 1 hour.

3 Preheat the oven to 180°C/350°F/Gas 4 and line a baking sheet with baking parchment.

4 On a lightly floured surface, roll out the dough to about 1cm/½in thick and cut into circles using a 10cm/4in cookie cutter. Put on the baking sheet.

5 Brush each pagace with beaten egg. Sprinkle with some sea salt and caraway seeds, then bake for 15–20 minutes, or until lightly golden. Cool on a wire rack. Serve with butter and cheese or as the base for a sandwich. They are also a good accompaniment to soup.

Serves 6

about 300g/11oz/scant 3 cups polohruba
   flour, or 300g/11oz/scant 3 cups plain
   (all-purpose) flour and 175g/6oz/1½
   cups semolina, plus extra for dusting
10ml/2 tsp baking powder
250ml/8fl oz/1 cup sour cream
pinch of salt
250g/9oz/generous 1 cup butter
115g/4oz/1 cup grated Edam cheese
1 egg, beaten
sea salt and caraway seeds, to sprinkle

PER SERVING: Energy 760kcal/3129kj; Protein 16; Carbohydrate 64g, of which sugars 3g; Fat 50g, of which saturates 30g; Cholesterol 166mg; Calcium 295mg; Fibre 2.9g; Sodium 703mg.

Serves 4

400g/14oz/3½ cups hruba flour, or
   250g/9oz/2¼ cups plain (all-purpose)
   flour and 150g/5oz/scant 1 cup
   semolina, plus extra for dusting
1 egg
250g/9oz/generous 1 cup tvaroh cheese
   mixed with 50g/2oz icing
   (confectioners') sugar, or quark and
   cottage cheese mixed with 50g/2oz
   icing sugar
1 egg yolk
65g/2½oz (50g/2oz plus 15g/½oz /1 tbsp)
   butter
40g/1½oz/scant 1 cup fine dried
   breadcrumbs
salt

Slovak Pirohy
Pirohy

This is a very popular Slovak dish, which has both sweet
and savoury versions. The sweet pirohy made here
contain a sweetened cheese filling and are topped with
melted butter and fried breadcrumbs.

1 Put the flour, or flour mixture, into a
large bowl. Using a fork, slowly blend
the egg and a pinch of salt into the
flour, adding cold water to make the
dough more pliable, if necessary. On a
floured surface, roll the dough out very
thinly, then cut into 4cm/1½in squares.

2 In a separate bowl mix the cheese
with the icing sugar and the egg yolk.
Spoon the filling into the middle of
each dough square, fold over the
dough and seal using your fingers or a
fork to crimp the edges.

3 Bring a large pan of water to the boil
and add a pinch of salt. Place the
pirohy into the water in small batches
of 5–8 so that they do not stick. Cook
for 6–7 minutes or until they rise.

4 Melt 50g/2oz/4 tbsp butter. Drain the
pirohy, put into a warmed bowl, then
pour over the melted butter. Fry the
breadcrumbs in 15g/½oz/1 tbsp butter
and add the remaining icing sugar.
Mix well and fry until crispy, for 2–3
minutes. Serve the pirohy warm with
the breadcrumbs and melted butter.

PER SERVING: Energy 611kcal/2581kj; Protein 21g; Carbohydrate 101g, of which sugars 17g; Fat 16g, of which saturates 9g; Cholesterol 86mg; Calcium 191mg; Fibre 4.2g; Sodium 311mg.

Serves 4

1 egg
300ml/½ pint/1¼ cups milk
50g/2oz/¼ cup vanilla sugar
15g/½oz/1 tbsp butter, melted
pinch of salt
200g/7oz/1¾ cups plain (all-purpose)
    flour
10ml/2 tsp baking powder
vegetable oil, for frying
strawberry jam and icing sugar, to serve

VARIATION

Serve with your own favourite toppings –
maple syrup, chocolate, sweetened curd
cheese (tvaroh) or blackcurrant jam.

COOK'S TIP

It is useful to have a crumpet pan to
make these, or you can use metal rings
(about 8cm/3in in diameter). Otherwise
simply use a frying pan.

Crumpets
Lívance/Lievance

These little crumpet-style pancakes are often eaten on
their own as a sweet main course, or served as an
accompaniment to lentil soup. They can also be served
as a delicious dessert.

1 To make the batter, beat the egg
with the milk and sugar, melted butter
and salt. Add the flour and baking
powder. Mix well and leave to rise for
10–15 minutes.

2 Heat a little vegetable oil in a frying
pan (pour about 5ml/1 tsp over the
pan with a pastry brush, very quickly
to avoid burning the brush).

3 Put 2–3 tablespoon-sized portions
of batter in the pan and cook over a
medium-low heat for 3–5 minutes on
each side. Allow enough space
between the crumpets so that they do
not touch. Generally the hotter the pan
the smaller the crumpets – aim for
7.5cm/3in in diameter or smaller.

4 If using rings to shape the crumpets,
put 2–3 rings on the greased preheated
pan at a time, put a portion of batter in
each one and leave for a few seconds
until the dough cooks on the bottom.
Remove the rings using oven mitts.
Serve with jam and icing sugar.

PER SERVING: Energy 368kcal/1547kj; Protein 9g; Carbohydrate 56g, of which sugars 17g; Fat 13g, of which saturates 5g; Cholesterol 76mg; Calcium 192mg; Fibre1.8g; Sodium 413mg.

Serves 4

100ml/3½fl oz/scant ½ cup ketchup
3 garlic cloves, peeled and crushed
400g/14oz/3½ cups plain (all-purpose)
    flour
about 350ml/12fl oz/1½ cups milk
40g/1½oz fresh yeast or 15g/½oz dry
    yeast
5ml/1 tsp salt
200ml/7fl oz/scant 1 cup oil
ketchup, garlic spread and 115g/4oz /
    1 cup grated Cheddar cheese, to serve
100ml/3½fl oz/scant ½ cup sour cream
    (optional)

COOK'S TIP
When working with the dough, put some
oil on your fingers to stop it sticking to
your hands.

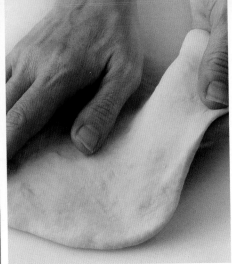

Langoš
Langoš

This recipe was originally Hungarian, made from bread
dough leftovers, but it is so popular in the Czech and Slovak
Republics that it has become part of their culture, too.

1 Combine the ketchup and garlic.
Sift the plain (all-purpose) flour into
a large bowl. Heat a 100ml/3½fl oz
scant ½ cup of the milk until tepid.
Crumble the fresh yeast into the milk
and whisk for 1 minute, then add to the
flour, or follow the instructions for
the dry yeast. Add the remaining milk.

2 Add the salt and mix to form a soft
dough; add more milk if the dough is
too hard to work with. Take a quarter
of the dough and stretch it out with
your hands into a flat pancake. (Or
divide it to make four little pancakes
for each quarter of dough.)

3 Preheat the oil in a frying pan. The
langoš is supposed to 'swim' in the
oil, so it needs to be about 2cm/¾in
deep. Fry the dough for 4–5 minutes on
each side, until golden, depending on
the size of the pancakes. Take care
as it is easy to burn them.

4 Transfer the langoš to kitchen
paper to drain. Serve hot with 45ml/
3 tbsp ketchup and garlic spread or
45ml/3 tbsp sour cream, and topped
with grated cheese.

PER SERVING: Energy 398kcal/2929kj; Protein 21g; Carbohydrate 92g, of which sugars 15g; Fat 30g, of which saturates 13g; Cholesterol 55mg; Calcium 483mg; Fibre 3.6g; Sodium 866mg.

Makes 15–20

20g/¾oz fresh yeast

15ml/1 tbsp caster (superfine) sugar

1.5 litres/2½ pints/6¼ cups whole milk, tepid

2.5ml/½ tsp salt

1 egg

300g/11oz/scant 3 cups polohruba flour, or 200g/7oz strong white bread flour and 100g/3¾oz/generous ½ cup semolina, sifted, plus extra for dusting

70g/3oz Svestkova Povidla/Slivkový Lekvár, or plum jam (page 20), or canned strawberries in syrup

75g/3oz/6 tbsp butter, melted

100g/3¾oz/generous ½ cup icing (confectioners') sugar

100g/3¾oz/generous ½ cup Granko or unsweetened cocoa powder

pinch of salt

Fruit Dumplings
Ovocné knedlíky/Ovocné buchty

These light, fluffy dumplings, a great favourite in both countries, are so filling that they are often eaten as a main dish, usually at lunchtime.

1 To activate the yeast, empty a sachet of dried yeast and the sugar into a jug (pitcher). Heat the milk until tepid, pour 100ml into the yeast and sugar and stir to dissolve. Cover with a cloth and place in a warm airing cupboard for 10–15 minutes. When the yeast is frothy, add ½ tsp salt to arrest the activation process and stir in.

2 Beat the egg into the remaining milk. Sift the flour mixture into a bowl and make a well. Mix the yeast with the flour using your hand. Add the egg and milk, adding sufficient to combine the dough into a ball. On a floured surface knead the dough for 3 minutes.

3 Put the dough ball into a clean, lightly floured bowl. Cover with a dish towel and put in a warm airing cupboard for half an hour until doubled.

4 Dust three baking sheets with flour and dust the work surface.

5 Using a sharp knife cut the dough into 15–20 equal pieces. Knead each lightly, then flatten out to a thin round.

6 Add 1 tsp of jam or drained fruit to the centre of each round, then fold the dough around the jam into a ball so there are no seams. Space wide apart on the sheets and put in a warm cupboard for 10 minutes until doubled.

7 Bring a large pan of water to the boil and add a pinch of salt. Put four or five dumplings at a time into the boiling water using a slotted spoon. Cook for 10 minutes, turning once half way through cooking.

8 Melt the butter and put in a bowl for dipping. Add the sifted icing sugar and cocoa powder to separate bowls.

9 Drain the dumplings and put on a warm plate. Top each one with the butter, the icing sugar and the cocoa.

PER SERVING: Energy kcal680/2862kj; Protein 18g; Carbohydrate 99g, of which sugars 39g; Fat 27g, of which saturates 15g; Cholesterol 108mg; Calcium212mg; Fibre 3.1g; Sodium 757mg.

Serves 4

1 litre/3¾ pints/4 cups milk

pinch of salt

115g–150g/4–5oz/generous ½– ¾ cup
caster (superfine) sugar, to taste

300g/11oz/1¾ cup semolina

For the butter topping

50g/2oz/¼ cup butter, melted

60ml/4 tbsp icing (confectioners') sugar

60ml/4 tbsp unsweetened cocoa powder

For the cinnamon and apple topping

60ml/4 tbsp icing (confectioners') sugar

4 tsp ground cinnamon

1 apple, cored and chopped or sliced

For the honey and nut topping

60ml/4 tbsp honey

60ml/4 tbsp ground or finely
chopped nuts

Sweet Semolina Pudding
Krupice/Krupica

This classic childhood favourite was often served as a light supper when I was little. It is also one of the easiest recipes to make – just remember to keep stirring the semolina while it is cooking.

1 Put the milk in a pan with the salt and sugar and heat to almost boiling. Add the semolina and stir until it thickens slightly. Cook for 4–5 minutes – the semolina is cooked when you feel it sticking to the base of the pan.

2 Serve hot, with your choice of topping. For the butter topping, pour over melted butter and sprinkle with icing sugar and cocoa.

3 For the cinnamon and apple topping, sprinkle with icing sugar and cinnamon, and top with chopped or sliced apple.

4 For the honey and nut topping, drizzle over the honey and sprinkle with ground or finely chopped nuts.

PER SERVING: Energy 816kcal/3434kj; Protein 20g; Carbohydrate 125g, of which sugars 66g; Fat 30g, of which saturates 14g; Cholesterol 62mg; Calcium 327mg; Fibre 4.4g; Sodium 340mg.

Serves 4

200g/7oz cup short grain rice, rinsed
1 cinnamon stick
600ml/1 pint/2½ cups milk
50g/2oz/¼ cup butter
30ml/2 tbsp vanilla sugar
5ml/1 tsp ground cinnamon
4 eggs, separated
100g/3¾oz cups caster sugar
100g/3¾oz fruit, such as apricots, plums, cherries or apples
50g/2oz dried raisins or sultanas (golden raisins)
100g/3¾oz, melted butter, and icing (confectioners') sugar, to serve

VARIATION

Use all the egg whites in the rice and sprinkle the finished dish with unsweetened cocoa powder.

Baked Rice Pudding
Sladká rýže/Sladká rýža

This sweet main course, used in both Republics, is another that children adore. Unlike the traditional English rice pudding, this includes fresh fruit, egg yolks and whisked egg whites, and is served with melted butter.

1 Put the rice in a pan, cover with water, add the cinnamon stick. Bring to the boil, cook for 10 minutes and drain.

2 Put the rice and cinnamon stick back into the pan and add milk to cover the rice. Bring to a gentle boil and cook until soft, stirring occasionally and adding more milk if necessary. Remove the cinnamon stick when cooked. Add the butter, vanilla sugar and ground cinnamon, and mix well. Cover and leave to cool for 3–4 minutes.

3 Preheat the oven to180°C/350°F/Gas 4 and grease a baking dish. Add the egg yolks to the rice and mix well. Put the egg whites into a clean, grease-free bowl and whisk until the meringue starts to stiffen.

4 Add 110g/ 3¾oz caster sugar and continue whisking until you have stiff peaks. Add three-quarters of the whites to the rice, then put the remainder in the refrigerator.

5 Remove the stones (pits) from stone fruits, if using, or core the apples. Halve the cherries or roughly chop the other fruits. Add the fruits and the raisins or sultanas and mix.

6 Transfer the rice to the baking dish and bake for 30 minutes, or until it has set – test by inserting a wooden cocktail stick (toothpick). Top with the remaining whipped egg whites and bake for a further 10 minutes. Serve hot, topped with melted butter and dusted with icing sugar.

PER SERVING: Energy 739kcal/3803kj; Protein 17g; Carbohydrate 69g, of which sugars 26g; Fat 46g, of which saturates 26g; Cholesterol 338mg; Calcium 232mg; Fibre 2.4g; Sodium 404mg.

Doughnuts with 'Snow'
Vdolky s pěnou/Dolky s penou

This delicious sweet recipe is traditional in both countries. In the Czech Republic they are served with plum jam and grated sweet cheese and in Slovakia with a sweet 'snow' made with caster sugar, egg whites, icing sugar and jam.

Serves 4

250ml/8fl oz/1 cup tepid milk
40ml/8 tsp caster (superfine) sugar
40g/1½oz fresh yeast or 15g/½oz dry
    yeast
500g polohruba flour (alternatively mix
    250g/9oz/generous 2 cups plain flour
    with 250g/9oz semolina)
pinch of salt
1 egg
2 egg yolks
90ml/6 tbsp vegetable oil
75ml/5 tbsp rum
200ml/7fl oz/scant 1 cup vegetable oil for
    shallow-frying, or oil for deep-frying

For the 'snow' topping

100g/3¾oz/generous ½ cup caster
    (superfine) sugar
2 egg whites
pinch of salt
100g/3¾oz/scant 1 cup icing
    (confectioners') sugar
about 75ml/5 tbsp sour red jam, or any
    red jam, such as strawberry

For the jam and cheese topping

50g/2oz plum jam (see page 20)
    or povidla
50g/2oz grated hard tvaroh, or quark and
    cottage cheese mixed

1 To make the dough, combine the milk with the caster sugar in a small bowl/mug and crumble in the yeast. Stir and leave to rise for 10–15 minutes.

2 In a large bowl mix together the flour, salt, egg, egg yolks, oil, rum and the prepared yeast mixture. Work the dough together using a wooden spoon. Cover with a clean dish towel and leave in a warm place to rise for 45 minutes.

3 In the meantime, make the 'snow' topping, if you have chosen to use this one. Put the caster sugar in a bowl and add 30ml/2 tbsp boiling water. Dissolve and leave to cool completely. Once cool, put the egg whites and salt into a clean, grease-free bowl and whisk until they form stiff peaks. Add the icing sugar and whisk until glossy. Keep beating with the electric mixer while trickling the sugar water into the egg whites. Gradually fold in the jam 15ml/1 tbsp one at a time.

4 When the dough has risen, cut out doughnut-sized balls using a tablespoon and form into doughnut shapes. Heat the oil in a frying pan or use a deep-fryer. Poke an indent into the middle of each piece of dough and stretch each doughnut sideways.

5 Fry until golden; 3–4 minutes each side, if using a frying pan. Lift out the doughnuts with a slotted spoon and drain on a piece of kitchen paper. Serve warm with your topping of choice.

COOK'S TIPS
• To make this process even simpler, use a home breadmaking machine to combine the dough.
• The dough can be made in advance and stored sealed in a plastic bag in the refrigerator for a couple of days.

PER SERVING: Energy 1050kcal/4419kj; Protein 21g; Carbohydrate 158g, of which sugars 61g; Fat 41g, of which saturates 7g; Cholesterol 69mg; Calcium 225mg; Fibre 4.7g; Sodium 228mg.

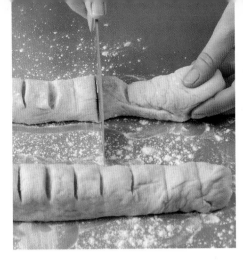  

Ducat Cakes
Dukátové buchtičky

This baked yeast cake recipe will provide a trip down memory lane for many Czech and Slovak compatriots. The dish, with its unusual combination of ingredients, is often on the menu in school kitchens and is an uplifting and satisfying meal. The vanilla pudding it is served with is similar to custard but with a more fluid texture.

Makes 20–25

250g/9oz/generous 2 cups polohruba
  flour, or 200g/7oz/1¾ cups plain flour
  and 50g/2oz/⅓ cup semolina, plus
  extra flour for dusting
2 sachets instant yeast
25g/1oz/2 tbsp butter, melted, plus extra
  for greasing
1 egg yolk
30ml/2 tbsp caster (superfine) sugar
2.5ml/½ tsp salt
5ml/1 tsp vanilla sugar
150ml/¼ pint/⅔ cup whole milk, tepid
115g/4oz/½ cup butter, melted

For the pudding

750ml/1¼pints/3 cups whole milk
3 egg yolks
20g/¾oz/1½ tbsp vanilla sugar,
  or to taste
40g/1½oz instant vanilla pudding powder
15ml/1 tbsp rum

1 Put the flour into a large bowl with the yeast, melted butter, egg yolk, caster sugar, salt, vanilla sugar and milk. Mix together with a wooden spoon and then use an electric mixer with a bread hook attachment or knead with your hands for 2–3 minutes.

2 Dust with flour, then cover with a dish towel and leave to stand in a warm place for 1 hour. Preheat the oven to 160°C/325°F/Gas 3 and grease a 18cm/7in round baking tin.

3 Dust your work surface with flour and turn out the dough. Work with your hands for 3 minutes, then divide the dough into two. Roll each half out into a long roll 50cm long by 2.5cm/1in thick. Using a sharp knife, roughly cut each roll into 10 pieces, then roll each one into a ball. Cover and allow to stand for a further 10 minutes.

4 Place one by one inside the baking dish, brushing each one all over with melted butter. Bake for 25 minutes. Leave to stand for 10 minutes before serving (the balls will stick together).

5 To make the pudding, whisk all the ingredients together in large heavy pan, then simmer over medium heat, stirring constantly, until the pudding thickens. Serve hot over the buns.

COOK'S TIPS
• Instant vanilla pudding powder is available in the foreign section of many high street supermarkets or in Polish delicatessens.
• If you can't find vanilla pudding powder, you can adapt the pudding cream instructions by combining 30g/1¼oz caster sugar and 125ml/4fl oz white wine in a bowl. Add 1 egg, 1 egg yolk and 1 tbsp freshly squeezed lemon juice. Whisk over steam (bain-marie) for 5 minutes. Alternatively, use bought vanilla pudding or vanilla custard.

PER SERVING: Energy 125kcal/512kj; Protein 3g; Carbohydrate 12g, of which sugars 5g; Fat 7g, of which saturates 4g; Cholesterol 49mg; Calcium 59mg; Fibre 0.4g; Sodium 69mg.

DESSERTS
& BAKING

There is no shortage of sweet recipes in the Czech Republic and Slovakia. However, because sweet dishes are often used as the main course, desserts are not automatically served as the finale to a meal. Those that are used in this way include Apple and Cinnamon Bread Pudding and Sweet Crêpes. Baking has a strong presence at all points of the day in both countries. Cakes are often eaten with tea or coffee for a breakfast, midmorning or teatime snack. Rye bread and rohlíky or rožky are both staples of the cuisine, and essential accompaniments to many meals.

Crêpes, koláče, mole's cake & rohlíky

If you like to have a sweet course to conclude a meal, then take your choice from Kremes, a delicious layered cream cake with puff pastry and custard cream, and Sweet Buns, or Koláče, where the dough is wrapped around the filling of cheese, jam, poppy seeds or breadcrumbs. Other desserts might use smaller helpings of some of the recipes in the previous chapter, such as Doughnuts with Snow or Ducat Cakes.

When it comes to baking, Czechs and Slovaks like to have sweet snacks throughout the day, and these include a variety of cakes. They include the generously fluffy Pound Cake (Babovka) or a temptingly moist Fruit Cake (Bublanina). Another example is the surprisingly named Mock Saddle of Venison Cake, of Austrian origin. So, instead of a meat dish there appears a cake baked in the shape of a venison loin, prepared with flour, butter, sugar, chocolate and walnuts. Another cake where the shape defines the name is Mole's Cake, a melt-in-the-mouth banana and cream cake imitating the shape of a mole hill. Little Mole, known as Krtek, Krtko, Krteček, or Krečík, is also an adored children's cartoon from the Socialist era, and in one of the episodes he is shown cooking koláče for his friend the frog's birthday. Christmas and celebration days will also involve households in busy baking preparations and the wafting sweet aromas of cakes such as Paška, or Easter Cake, will permeate the whole house.

Bread is a basic staple in both countries. Often a thick slice will be served for breakfast with a sweet or savoury topping, perhaps with some ham for a mid-morning snack. Bread components also frequently feature in other dishes, or provide essential accompaniments. In Slovakia, black bread or rye bread is a remnant of the long period of domination by the Austro-Hungarian Empire. Rohlíky or rožky are soft white rolls that are unique to the Czech Republic and Slovakia. They are an essential part of a street food called párek v rohlíku or rožku, a frankfurter sausage buried inside a rohlík or rožok and served with an indulgent coating of ketchup or mustard.

Serves 3–4

200g/7oz/generous 1⅔ cups plain
  (all-purpose) flour
2 eggs
pinch of salt
500ml/17fl oz/2¼ cups milk
butter or oil, for frying

For the topping and filling

100g/3¾oz chocolate spread or
  blackcurrant jam
1 can of strawberries in syrup
  (400g/14oz can)
100g/3¾oz icing (confectioners') sugar
whipped cream, to serve
chocolate topping/syrup (in bottle)

Sweet Crêpes
Palačinky/Palacinky

This dish is eaten as a dessert and as a main course.
Each serving consists of one large, thin pancake, spread
with the filling, then rolled up and topped with icing
sugar, whipped cream and chocolate.

1 Combine the flour and eggs in a
bowl. Add the salt and gradually add
the milk while whisking the batter.
The mixture should be the
consistency of double (heavy) cream;
if it is too thin, add more flour,
and if it is too thick, add more milk.

2 Heat a small amount of butter or
oil in a non-stick frying pan over
medium heat. Pour a ladleful of
batter into the pan and spread it
evenly by moving the pan from side
to side. Cook for about 2–3 minutes
until golden underneath, then flip the
pancake over and cook on the other
side. Remove and keep warm while
you make the other pancakes.

3 Spread half of the pancakes with
chocolate spread or jam and roll
them up. Sprinkle with icing sugar,
then decorate with whipped cream
and chocolate topping. For the rest of
the pancakes, place 5–6 strawberries
in the middle and roll them up. To
serve, dust with icing sugar and
top with whipped cream and the
chocolate topping.

PER SERVING: Energy 644kcal/2707kj; Protein 14; Carbohydrate 89g, of which sugars 51g; Fat 28g, of which saturates 5g; Cholesterol 84mg; Calcium 239mg; Fibre 2.0g; Sodium 201mg.

Makes 3

250g/9oz/generous 1 cup butter,
  softened
250g/9oz/generous 1 cup sour cream
30ml/2 tbsp sugar
15ml/1 tsp vanilla essence
large pinch of salt
250g/9oz/2¼ cups plain (all-purpose) flour
icing (confectioners') sugar, sifted, for
  dusting

For the filling

2–3 cooking apples
45–60ml/3–4 tbsp sultanas (golden
  raisins) or raisins
45ml/3 tbsp light muscovado
  (brown) sugar
115g/4oz/1 cup walnuts, roughly chopped
5–10ml/1–2 tsp ground cinnamon
60ml/4 tbsp apricot jam or conserve

Apple Strudel with Raisins
Jablečný štrůdl/Jablkova' štrúdľa

This crisp pastry roll, filled with apples, raisins, sultanas
and apricot jam, is a classic after-dinner sweet treat. It
is delicious served with a scoop of vanilla ice cream or a
serving of whipped cream and a sprinkling of icing sugar.

1 To make the pastry, beat the butter until it is light and fluffy, then add the sour cream, sugar, vanilla essence and salt, and beat the contents together well.

2 Stir the flour into the mixture, then put in a plastic bag and chill overnight or longer.

3 Preheat the oven to 180°C/350°F/ Gas 4. To make the filling, core and finely chop the apples but do not peel.

4 Put the apples in a bowl, add the sultanas or raisins, sugar, walnuts, cinnamon and apricot jam or conserve and mix everything together until it is well combined.

5 Divide the pastry into three equal pieces. Place one piece on a sheet of lightly floured greaseproof (waxed) paper and roll out to a rectangle measuring about 45–30cm/18–12in.

6 Spread one-third of the filling over the pastry, leaving a 1–2cm/½–¾in border. Roll up the pastry to enclose the filling and place, seam-side down, on a non-stick baking sheet. Repeat with the remaining pastry and filling. Bake the strudels for 25–30 minutes until golden brown all over.

7 Remove the strudels from the oven and leave for 5 minutes to become slightly firm, then cut into slices. Cool, then dust with icing sugar.

PER SERVING: Energy 525kcal/2207kJ; Protein 8.9g; Carbohydrate 69.6g, of which sugars 41g; Fat 24.9g, of which saturates 11.6g; Cholesterol 195mg; Calcium 151mg; Fibre 3.1g; Sodium 228mg.

Serves 4–6

200g/7oz white bread slices, crust
   removed
150ml/¼ pint/⅔ cup single (light) cream
50g/2oz/¼ cup butter, melted
4 eggs, separated
45ml/3 tbsp caster (superfine) sugar
200g/7oz sliced dried apples, chopped
50g/2oz/scant ½ cup raisins
2 teaspoons of cinnamon
75g/2oz/¼ cup flaked (sliced) almonds

Apple & Cinnamon Bread Pudding
Žemlovka

This classic recipe is comfort food at its very best. The dish would often be served in huge
portions for a main course on meatless Fridays. In modern kitchens, smaller portions are
served as a dessert accompanied by a scoop of ice cream or vanilla pudding.

1 Preheat the oven to 180°C/350°F/
Gas 4 and grease a 15 x 20cm/6 x 8in
ovenproof dish. Process the bread in
a food processor or blender until you
have breadcrumbs. Transfer into a
bowl and add the cream and butter,
mixing well.

2 In another bowl, whisk the egg yolks
and sugar until light and creamy. Fold
the apples, raisins and cinnamon into
the whisked egg and sugar mix. Add
this to the breadcrumb mixture, and
combine well.

3 Put the egg whites into a clean,
grease-free bowl and whisk until they
form stiff peaks. Stir a spoonful of the
whites into the breadcrumb mixture to
lighten it, then fold in the remaining
whites. Pour into the prepared dish.

4 Sprinkle with the almonds and bake
for 25–30 minutes, or until it is golden
and firm.

VARIATION
Adding a grated apple to the dry apple
and raisin mixture makes the pudding
even more moist.

PER SERVING: Energy 379kcal/1585kJ; Protein 10.6g; Carbohydrate 34.9g, of which sugars 19g; Fat 23g, of which saturates 9.2g; Cholesterol 160mg; Calcium 119mg; Fibre 2.1g; Sodium 303mg.

Serves 4

800ml/27fl oz/scant 3¼ cups milk

100g/3¾oz instant vanilla pudding or
    vanilla custard powder

300g icing (confectioners') sugar

20g/¾oz vanilla sugar

3 egg yolks

15ml/1 tbsp rum

40ml/2 heaped tbsp flour

400g/14oz puff pastry, thawed if frozen

2.5ml/½ tsp gelatine

500ml/17fl oz/generous 2 cups double
    (heavy) cream

50g/2oz icing (confectioners') sugar
    for dusting

COOK'S TIP

It is best to leave the cake in the
refrigerator overnight; this will make it
more stable and easier to cut.

Kremes

Kremeš/Krémeš

This rich cream cake is a Slovak dish. Some recipes use
a digestive-biscuit base, others put puff pastry on top
and underneath, and some also add melted chocolate.

1 Pour the milk into a pan and add the
custard powder, 200g of icing sugar,
vanilla sugar, egg yolks, rum and flour.

2 Beat using an electric mixer, then
put over medium heat and cook,
beating, until the mixture becomes
very thick. Leave to cool. Preheat the
oven to 200°C/400°F/Gas 6.

3 Split the puff pastry into two halves
and roll them out to dimensions of
30 x 20cm/12 x 8in and lift on to a
baking sheet. Bake for 20–30 minutes.
Leave to cool.

4 Put 15ml/1 tbsp cold water into a
small heatproof bowl or cup and
sprinkle the gelatine over. Soak for
5 minutes, then put the bowl or cup
into a pan of hot water until dissolved.

5 Whip the cream with the rest of the
icing sugar until almost stiff, then add
the gelatine. Continue whipping the
cream until it forms stiff peaks. Spread
the custard cream on to one half of the
cooled puff pastry, and top with the
whipped cream. Cover with the other
half and dust with icing sugar. Chill for
at least 2–3 hours before serving.

PER SERVING: Energy 1668kcal/6966kj; Protein 18g; Carbohydrate 176g, of which sugars 109g; Fat 104g, of which saturates 48g; Cholesterol 351mg; Calcium 395mg; Fibre 2.7g; Sodium 524mg.

Serves 4

250ml/7fl oz/scant 1 cup milk

80g/3oz caster (superfine) sugar

30g/1¼oz yeast (fresh is best but you can
    use instant – substitute 2 sachets)

500g/1¼lb plain flour, sifted, plus extra
    for dusting

50g/2oz butter, melted but cooled

2 egg yolks, whisked

pinch of salt

1 egg for glazing, whisked

Cheese topping:

250g/9oz Tvaroh (or substitute Quark or
    other curd cheese)

45ml/3 tbsp vanilla sugar

50g/2oz icing (confectioners') sugar

1 egg yolk

20g/¾oz butter

pinch of lemon rind

dried raisins

Jam topping:

50g/2oz butter

100g/3¾oz icing (confectioners') sugar

50g/2oz plain flour or dried breadcrumbs

150g/5oz Povidla (or substitute plum
    jam)

Poppy seed topping:

300g/11oz ground poppy seeds

50g/2oz icing (confectioner's) sugar

50ml/3½ tbsp milk

For the breadcrumb topping

25g/1oz/2 tbsp butter

65g/2½oz/generous ½ cup icing
    (confectioners') sugar

50g/2oz/½ cup plain (all-purpose) flour

Sweet Buns
Koláče

These round sweet buns – pronounced ko-lah-cheh – are a Czech recipe. The four toppings here are cheese with raisins, plum jam, poppy seeds, and breadcrumbs.

1 Warm 100ml/3¾oz of the milk in a small pan. Then add a tablespoon of caster sugar and crumble in the yeast. Whisk together, cover and leave to activate and rise for 10 minutes.

2 Sift the flour into a bowl, add the butter, egg yolks, salt, the remaining milk and caster sugar and the activated yeast. Mix together using a wooden spoon for 5 minutes. Dust with flour, cover with a tea towel and leave to rise for 2 hours – until it has doubled in size.

3 In the meantime prepare the toppings – for the cheese topping mix all of the ingredients together; for the jam topping, heat the butter in a pan, add the sugar and breadcrumbs (or flour) and mix until you get a crumble texture; for the poppy seed topping bring the milk to the boil, add sugar and poppy seeds and cook for 3 minutes and leave to cool, this is sprinkled on top of the Povidla.

4 When the dough is ready, use a tablespoon to cut out large pieces and place them on a floured surface. Roll each one in a ball about 4–5cm/1½–2in diameter and pat it down to make a pancake roughly 2cm/¾in thick. Make an indent in the middle of each one where the topping will sit.

5 Spoon roughly a tablespoon of each topping on to a third of the koláče. Use all of the toppings you have providing generous servings. When using the Povidla, top this with the breadcrumb topping. Glaze each koláče with an egg.

6 Bake in a preheated oven at 180ºC/350ºF/Gas 4 for about 20–25 minutes until golden. Leave to cool and serve.

COOK'S TIP

If you're using the plum topping, try to get the real povidla/slivkoỷ lekvár plum jam, as this is a different consistency from most jams, more like a plum compôte.

PER SERVING: Energy 1313kcal/5540kj; Protein 30g; Carbohydrate 230g, of which sugars 30g; Fat 36g, of which saturates 20g; Cholesterol 287mg; Calcium 412mg; Fibre 6.1g; Sodium 489mg.

Poppy Seed or Walnut Roll
Makovník a ořechovník/Makovník a orechovník

Serves 4

150ml/¼ pint/⅔ cup milk
25g/1oz fresh yeast, or 1 sachet active dried yeast
45ml/3 tbsp icing (confectioners') sugar
300g/11oz/scant 3 cups plain (all-purpose) flour, plus extra for dusting
5ml/1 tsp baking powder
1 egg, beaten
pinch of salt
50g/2oz/¼ cup unsalted butter, softened
15ml/1 tbsp oil, plus extra for greasing
1 egg yolk, beaten

For the poppy seed filling

150–200g/5–7oz ground poppy seeds
115g/4oz/1 cup icing (confectioners') sugar, or to taste
50–100ml/2–3½fl oz/¼–scant ½ cup milk

For the walnut filling

150–200g/5–7oz walnuts, crushed
115g/4oz/1 cup icing (confectioners') sugar, or to taste
50–100ml/2–3½fl oz/¼–scant ½ cup milk

This is a classic teatime cake with either a poppy seed or walnut filling, and is loved in both countries. A Slovak alternative, called tvarožník, uses a sweet curd cheese spread on the dough instead of rolled up inside it.

1 Warm up the milk, pour it into a bowl and add the yeast and 15ml/1 tbsp icing sugar. Whisk. Cover and leave in a warm place for 10–15 minutes, until frothy.

2 Sift the flour and baking powder into a bowl. Stir in the remaining icing sugar, the egg, salt, butter and yeast. Gather the dough together (add cold water if you feel it is too solid). Knead on a floured surface until the dough comes away from the bowl sides.

3 Pat the dough into the bowl and dust with flour. Cover and leave in a warm place for 30 minutes to 1 hour, until doubled in size. Grease a baking tray and preheat the oven to 160°C/325°F/Gas 3.

4 Prepare your choice of filling. Mix the poppy seeds or walnuts with the icing sugar, according to taste. Add enough milk to make a thick, spreading consistency.

5 When the dough is ready, roll and pat it out on a floured work surface. Spread the oil evenly over the dough and then top with your choice of filling. Roll up the dough, then transfer it carefully to the baking tray keeping the dough fold underneath.

6 Brush the top with egg yolk to glaze it. Pierce the roll with a fork in a couple of places and bake for 25–30 minutes. Transfer to a wire rack and leave to cool before serving.

PER AVERAGE SERVING: Energy 898kcal/3763kj; Protein 18g; Carbohydrate 99g, of which sugars 41g; Fat 50g, of which saturates 12g; Cholesterol 145mg; Calcium 242mg; Fibre 5.3g; Sodium 274mg.

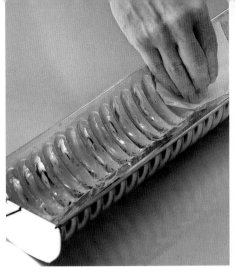

Makes 10 slices
115g/4oz/½ cup butter, softened, plus extra for greasing
50g/2oz/½ cup icing (confectioners') sugar
35g/1½oz/3 tbsp vanilla sugar
3 eggs, separated
5ml/1 tsp baking powder
115g/4oz/1 cup polohruba flour, or 70g/3oz/⅔ cup plain (all-purpose) flour and 30g/1¼oz/scant ½ cup semolina, plus extra for dusting
100g/3¾oz crushed walnuts
pinch of salt
65g/2½oz dark (bittersweet) chocolate, coarsely grated
45ml/3 tbsp rum
icing (confectioners') sugar for dusting

Mock Saddle of Venison Cake
Srnčí hřbet/Srnčí chrbát

This recipe is of Austrian descent. It is common in Czech Moravia, made in a Rehrucken pan, a ribbed loaf pan. This walnut saddle of venison has the same name as the recipe made with meat, so its arrival can surprise guests!

1 Preheat the oven to 180°C/350°F/Gas 4. Grease a 30 x 10cm/12 x 4in Rehrucken pan or Moravian loaf tin (pan), or use a 28 x 10cm/11 x 4in loaf tin.

2 Put the butter into a bowl and beat in the icing sugar and vanilla sugar using an electric whisk, until creamy, then beat in the egg yolks.

3 Sift the baking powder and flour, or flour mixture, over the creamed mixture, then gradually fold it into the butter and sugar, with the walnuts, salt, chocolate and rum. Stir well.

4 Put the egg whites into a clean, grease-free bowl and whisk until they form stiff peaks. Gently fold this into the cake batter. Spoon into the prepared cake tin.

5 Bake for 18–20 minutes, or until golden on the outside and an inserted skewer comes out clean. Leave in the tin on a wire rack for 15 minutes before turning out. Leave to cool and dust with icing sugar.

PER SERVING: Energy 289kcal/1204kj; Protein 5g; Carbohydrate 23g, of which sugars 13g; Fat 20g, of which saturates 8g; Cholesterol 71mg; Calcium 38mg; Fibre1.0g; Sodium 136mg.

Makes 20

butter, for greasing

165g/5½oz/generous 1¼ cups flour, plus
extra for dusting

4 eggs, separated

100ml/3½fl oz/scant ½ cup oil

100ml/3½fl oz/scant ½ cup milk

65g/2½oz/5 tbsp vanilla sugar

150g/5oz/1¼ cups icing (confectioners')
sugar

15ml/1 tbsp baking powder

200g/7oz fruit of choice, such as
peaches, apricots, cherries,
blackcurrants or plums – only use one
type of fruit and if using the larger
examples, halve them

COOK'S TIP

Any sort of canned fruit will also work
well in this cake.

Fruit Cake
Bublanina

In translation this fruit cake is called bubble cake.
This is because of the way the cake rises around the
fruit. It is delicious, quick and easy to make, usually
using whatever fruit is available.

1 Grease a 40.5 x 26.5 x 5cm (16 x 10
x 2in) baking tin (or line with non-
stick baking parchment), then
sprinkle with flour and shake the tray
to spread it evenly. Preheat the oven to
180°C/350°F/Gas 4.

2 Put the egg yolks into a bowl and add
the oil, milk, vanilla sugar and icing
sugar. Using an electric mixer, beat
the mixture for 2 minutes.

3 Sift the flour with the baking
powder and gradually add to the egg
mixture, beating between additions.

4 Put the egg whites into a clean,
grease-free bowl and whisk until they
form stiff peaks. Add a spoonful of
the whites to lighten the batter, then
fold in the remainder.

5 Pour the batter into the baking tray
and top with the fruit halves. Bake for
20 minutes, or until a wooden skewer
inserted into the centre comes out
clean. Transfer to a wire rack to cool.
Sift icing sugar over the top of the
cake before cutting into squares.

PER SERVING: Energy 140kcal/589kj; Protein 3g; Carbohydrate 19g, of which sugars 12g; Fat 7g, of which saturates 1g; Cholesterol 47mg; Calcium 28 mg; Fibre 0.5g; Sodium 44mg.

Serves 4
175g/6oz butter, melted, plus extra
   butter for greasing
30ml/2 tbsp dry breadcrumbs
4 eggs, separated
500g/1¼lb/generous 2½ cups caster
   (superfine) sugar
500ml/17½ fl oz/2 cups milk
15ml/1 tbsp baking powder
500g/1¼lb/5 cups plain (all-purpose)
   flour
icing (confectioners') sugar for dusting

Pound Cake
Bábovka

The traditional Czech form of the pound cake has
ripples, which also make it easier to decide on portion
sizes! This is a lovely light cake, and is delightful served
with afternoon tea.

VARIATION
You can experiment with ingredients by
adding sultanas (golden raisins), chopped
walnuts or a little lemon rind to the dough.

1 Preheat the oven to 150°C/300°F/
Gas 2. Grease a 450g/1lb cake tin
(pan) and use the breadcrumbs to
cover the side by sprinkling them into
the pan and shaking it to distribute
them. Using an electric mixer, beat
the egg yolks with half the sugar. Beat
in the milk and the remaining sugar.

2 Stir in the melted butter, sift the
baking powder and flour over the
mixture and stir. Pour the cake batter
into the tin and bake for 30–40
minutes, or until a wooden skewer
inserted in the centre comes out
clean. Cool for 5 minutes then
remove from the tin and leave to cool
completely. Dust with icing sugar.

VARIATION
To create a marbled effect, separate
the cake batter into three parts, add
15–30ml/1–2 tbsp cocoa powder to one-
third of the batter, then slowly pour a
third of the light-coloured mixture into
the cake tin followed by the darker
mixture and finally one-third of light
mixture. For extra marbling, use a metal
skewer to swirl the mixture around.

PER SERVING: Energy 1365kcal/5758k; Protein 21g; Carbohydrate 236g, of which sugars 134g; Fat 44g, of which saturates 25g; Cholesterol 325mg; Calcium 275mg; Fibre 3.9g; Sodium 772mg.

Mole's Cake
Krtkův dort/Krtkova torta

This delicious banana and cream cake is named after the shape that it resembles – a molehill! It is delightful when homemade and needs to be served chilled.

Makes 8

100g/3¾oz/scant 1 cup chocolate blancmange powder (alternatively use 3 tbsp cocoa powder mixed with 1 cup corn starch)

5ml/1 tsp baking powder

100g/3¾oz/scant 1 cup icing (confectioners') sugar

6 leaves of gelatine

2 eggs

100ml/3½fl oz/scant ½ cup oil

600ml/1 pint/2½ cups whipping cream

4 ripe bananas

65g/2½oz dark (bittersweet) chocolate chips

1 Preheat the oven to 180°C/350°F/Gas 4, and grease and flour a 25cm/10in round cake tin (pan). Mix the pudding powder (cocoa powder), baking powder and 75g/3oz /¾ cup icing (confectioners') sugar in a bowl.

2 Add the eggs and oil, and beat using an electric mixer for 3 minutes. Pour the batter into the cake tin and bake for 20 minutes or until a wooden skewer comes out clean. Cool for 5 minutes, then turn out of the tin and leave to cool completely.

3 Put 15ml/1 tbsp cold water into a small heatproof bowl or cup and sprinkle the gelatine over. Soak for 5 minutes, then put the bowl or cup into a pan of hot water until dissolved. Whip the cream until almost stiff, then add the gelatine. Continue whipping the cream until it forms stiff peaks.

4 Purée 1 banana in a separate bowl using an electric mixer. Add the remaining icing sugar to the whipped cream with the puréed banana and chocolate chips. Chill for 30 minutes.

5 When the cake is cool, use a knife and spoon to cut out the centre of the cake 1cm/½in deep, leaving a 1cm/½in margin. Put the removed cake into a bowl and crumble it into smaller pieces.

6 Cut the remaining bananas lengthways to make two halves from each. Lay these face down alongside each other inside the cake cavity. Scoop the cream filling on top, arranging it into a molehill shape, so that the middle is higher than the edge. Top the cream with the crumbs you have made, coating it completely. Leave to chill in the refrigerator for 1–2 hours and serve cold.

PER SERVING: Energy 610kcal/2530kj; Protein 5g; Carbohydrate 40g, of which sugars 36g; Fat 49g, of which saturates 25g; Cholesterol 137mg; Calcium 68mg; Fibre 1.7g; Sodium 240mg.

Slovak Easter Bread
Paška

This is eaten in Slovakia on Easter Sunday. A similar bread is made in the Czech Republic, decorated with raisins and almonds. Serve with cold meats, cheese and butter.

1 Grease a 20cm/8in round cake tin (pan) or a round baking dish. Mix 100ml/3½fl oz/scant ½ cup tepid milk with 15ml/1 tbsp caster sugar in a mug. Crumble in the fresh yeast and gradually stir in 15ml/1 tbsp flour. Mix well. Cover with a dish towel and put in a warm place for 10-15 minutes. The mixture should rise.

2 In a large bowl mix together the remaining flour, or flour mixture, caster sugar, vanilla sugar, salt and butter, then add the yeast mixture.

3 Beat the egg yolks, individually, into the remaining milk, then add this to the flour mixture.

4 Stir the dough with a wooden spoon, transfer to a floured work surface, knead for 5 minutes and form into a large round ball.

5 Return the dough to the bowl, dust with flour and cover with a dish towel. Put in a warm place for 1–2 hours, or until the dough rises. Preheat the oven to 180°C/350°F/Gas 4.

6 Put the dough into the prepared cake tin and leave to rest for 15 minutes. Cut a cross on top, brush with the beaten egg and bake for 35–40 minutes. The bread is cooked when a skewer comes out clean, or if it sounds hollow if you tap the base.

Serves 4

115g/4oz/½ cup butter, diced, plus extra for greasing
200ml/7fl oz/scant 1 cup whole milk, tepid
75g/3oz/6 tbsp caster (superfine) sugar
20g/¾oz fresh yeast or 7.5g/¼oz dry yeast
400g/14oz/3½ cups polohruba flour, or 300g/11oz/2¾ strong white bread flour and 115g/4oz/⅔ cup semolina, sifted, plus extra for dusting
20g/¾oz/1½ tbsp vanilla sugar
pinch of salt
3 egg yolks
1 egg, beaten

COOK'S TIP

You can experiment with the shape of your bread by separating the dough into three pieces before you let it rise, then braid the pieces and bake.

PER SERVING: Energy 765kcal/3214kj; Protein 16g; Carbohydrate 108g, of which sugars 28g; Fat 33g, of which saturates 18g; Cholesterol 277mg; Calcium 203mg; Fibre 3.7g; Sodium 240mg.

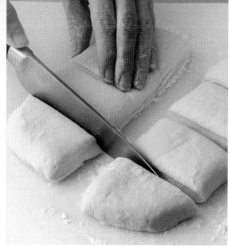

Rye Bread & Rohlíky or Rožky
Chléb/Chlieb & Rohlíky/Rožky

These two breads are central to both everyday cuisines, accompanying soups and main courses and mayonnaise-based salads, eaten as breakfast bread and rolls with yogurt, butter or ham. The rohlíky are also served as a street food with mustard, ketchup and a frankfurter.

Makes 1 loaf
For the bread
50ml/2fl oz/¼ cup milk, tepid
2.5ml/½ tsp caster (superfine) sugar
40g/1½oz fresh yeast, or 15g/½oz active dried yeast
250g/9oz/generous 2 cups strong white bread flour, plus extra for dusting
250g/9oz/generous 2 cups rye flour
5ml/1 tsp salt
5ml/1 tsp caraway seeds
250ml/8fl oz/1 cup water, tepid
15ml/1 tbsp white vinegar (distilled 8% vinegar)
butter, for greasing

Makes 16
For the rohlíky/rožky
20g/¾oz fresh yeast, or 7.5g/¼oz active dried yeast
5ml/1 tsp caster (superfine) sugar
300ml/½ pint/1¼ cups whole milk, tepid
500g/1¼lb/5 cups strong white bread flour
75g/3oz/6 tbsp lard or white cooking fat, softened, or butter
10ml/2 tsp salt
1 egg, beaten
butter, for greasing

TO MAKE THE RYE BREAD

1 In a small bowl, mix the milk and caster sugar, crumble in the fresh yeast and gradually stir in 15ml/1 tbsp bread flour. Cover with a dish towel and leave in a warm place for 10-15 minutes to become frothy.

2 Put the remaining ingredients in a large bowl, then add the yeast mixture. Mix with an electric mixer with a dough hook attachment or knead for 5 minutes. Cover and leave in a warm place to rise for 2 hours or until doubled in size.

3 On a floured work surface, knead the dough for 5 minutes. Return to the bowl, cover and leave in a warm place for 30 minutes, or until the dough rises again. Preheat the oven to 200°C/400°F/Gas 6 and grease a 30cm/12in oval baking dish.

4 Return the dough to the surface, shape into an oval, then put into the greased baking dish. Brush with cold water and bake for 20 minutes, then brush with water once again and reduce the oven temperature to 150°C/300°F/Gas 2. Bake for 30 minutes, or until the loaf has a dark golden brown crust. Remove and cool.

TO MAKE THE ROHLÍKY/ROŽKY

1 Crumble the yeast in a bowl with the sugar. Gradually add 100ml/3½fl oz/scant ½ cup tepid milk. Cover and leave in a warm place for 10 minutes until frothy.

2 Put the remaining ingredients, except the egg, into a large bowl and add the yeast mixture. Mix the ingredients with an electric mixer with dough hook attachment or knead for 5 minutes. Cover and leave in a warm place to rise for 30 minutes. Preheat the oven to180°C/350°F/Gas 4 and grease a baking sheet.

3 Divide the dough into two. Roll out each piece into a square 3cm/1¼in thick. Cut each into eight equal squares and roll each from corner to corner into a roll. Cover and leave to stand for 15 minutes. Put on to the baking sheet, brush with egg and bake for 15 minutes, or until very light golden brown and crisp. Cool.

RYE BREAD PER LOAF: Energy 1736kcal/7390kj; Protein 51g; Carbohydrate 383g, of which sugars 8g; Fat 10g, of which saturates 3g; Cholesterol 7mg; Calcium 490mg; Fibre 9.3g; Sodium 1997mg.
ROHLIKS/ROZOKS PER ROLL: Energy 168kcal/705kj; Protein 5g; Carbohydrate 25g, of which sugars 2g; Fat 6g, of which saturates 3g; Cholesterol 21mg; Calcium 68mg; Fibre 1.2g; Sodium 260mg.

Useful addresses

As well as those listed below, there is an extensive list of suppliers and restaurants specializing in the food of the Czech Republic and Slovakia on www.csplanet.com

AUSTRALIA

Czechoslovakian Club
25 Upfield Street
Burbank,
QLD 4156
T: (+61) (0)7 3343 3489
www.csklubqld.org.au

Czechoslovak Club in SA Inc.
51 Coglin Street
Brompton
SA 5007
T: (+61) (0)8 8346 4181
www.csclubsa.com

Tommy's European Beer Café
123 Glebe Point Rd
Glebe
NSW 2037
T: (+61) (0)2 9660 6870
tommysbeercafe.com.au

CANADA

Bohemia Restaurant
1725, Chemin des Prairies,
Brossard, Québec J4X 1G5
T: (+1) 450 444 5464
www.bohemiaresto.com

The Prague Fine Food
  Emporium
638 Queen Street West,
Toronto, ON M6J 1E4
T: (+1) 416 504 5787
www.theprague.ca

Prague Restaurant
450 Scarborough Golf Club Rd
Toronto
Ontario M1G 1H1
T: (+1) 416 289 0283
praguerestaurant.com

CZECH REPUBLIC

Boneco A.S.
Antusakova 266
256 36 Benesov
www.boneco.cz
Online shop with Czech
products

Konirna Restaurant
Maltezske namesti 10,
Lesser Town, Prague 1
www.konirna.eu

Novomestsky Pivovar
  Restaurant & Brewery
Vodickova 20, New Town,
Prague 1
www.npivovar.cz

Staromacek Restaurant
Karlova 46, Old Town
Prague 1
www.staromacek.cz

SLOVAKIA

Butterfly
Panska 8, Bratislava

Tempus Fugit
Sedlarska 5, Bratislava

UNITED KINGDOM

Czech and Slovak Club
74 West End Lane
West Hampstead
London NW6 2LX
T: (+44) (0)20 7372 1193
www.czechoslovak-
restaurant.co.uk

Dukla
19a Russell Parade
Golders Green Road
London NW11 9NN
T: (+44) (0)20 8458 1175
www.dukla.co.uk

Moya Slovak Restaurant
  and Bar
97 St. Clement's Street
Oxford OX4 1AR
T: (+44) (0)1865 200111
www.moya-oxford.co.uk

The Sonam Halusky Shop
132 Upper Richmond Rd West
East Sheen
London SW14 8DS
T: (+44) (0)20 8876 8346
www.halusky.co.uk

Tatra Eastern Corner
1 Newport Place
Northampton Street
Leicester
LE1 1DL
T: (+44) (0)7883 518180
www.tatraeasterncorner.co.uk

USA

American Czech-Slovak Club
13325 Arch Creek Road
North Miami
FL 33181
T: (+011) 305 891 9130
acscc.org

Andrusha
1370 Lexington Ave
New York
NY 10028
T: (+011) 212 369 9374

Bavarian Inn Restaurant
325 West Van Buren
Eureka Springs
Arkansas 72632
T: (+011) 479 253 8128
restaurant.eurekaspringsinn.c
om

Bohemian Garden
980 West 75th St.
Downers Grove
IL 60516
T: (+011) 630 960 0078
bohemian-garden.com

Cafe Prague
2 West 19th Street
Manhattan
New York
NY 10011
T: (+011) 212 929 2602
cafepraguenyc.com

Continental Bakery
119 Main Street
Everett
MA 02149
T: (+011) 617 387 4045
www.continentalbakery.com

Czech Stop & Little
  Czech Bakery
104 S George Kacir Dr,
West
TX 76691
T: (+011) 254 826 4161
www.czechstop.net

Dumpling Villa
300 E. St. Charles Road
Villa Park
IL 60181
T: (+011) 630 834 9565

European Deli
260 South Main Street
Manville
NJ 08835
T: (+011) 908 526 8972
http://www.europeandeli.net

J & T European Gourmet Food
1128 Wilshire Blvd
Santa Monica
CA 90401
T: (+011) 310 394 7227
www.jandtdeli.com

New Prague Restaurant
511 Rose Street
Georgetown, CO 80443
T: (+011) 303 569 2861

Old Prague Restaurant
5586 Liberty Avenue
Vermilion, OH 44089
T: (+011) 440 967 7182
oldprague.com

Schnitzel House
16150 SE 82nd Dr.
Clackamas
Oregon 97015
T: (+011) 503 657 3388

Slovak and Czech Store
10-59 Jackson Ave.
Long Island City
NY 11101
T: (+011) 718 752 2093
www.slovczechvar.com

Yukon Czech Hall
205 N Czech Hall Rd
Yukon
OK 73085
T: (+011) 405 324 8073
www.czechhall.com
Home of the finest Czech music
in Oklahoma

Index

A
alcohol 14–15
apples
  apple & cinnamon bread
    pudding 114
  apple strudel with raisins 113
  sweet semolina pudding 102

B
bacon 55
  potato dumplings with pork
    crackling 51
  potato pasta 86
  red pepper chicken paprikas
    61
  Spanish birds 81
baked potatoes with cream 91
baked rice pudding 103
baked trout with caraway 58
baking 109, 111
bananas
  mole's cake 122
beans
  sour bean soup 26
beef
  beef broth with dumplings 31
  beef goulash 77
  beef with dill sauce 80
  goulash soup 32
  roast beef in creamy sauce 76
  Spanish birds 81
  stuffed cabbage leaves 78
berries 20
black pudding soup 33
bread
  apple & cinnamon bread
    pudding 114
  bread dumplings 13
  fried bread with spicy
    stir-fry 49
  langos 100
  rye bread & rohlíky or rozky
    124

Slovak Easter bread 123
  sweet buns 116
butter
  potato skubanky 73
  sweet semolina pudding 102

C
cabbage
  roast goose with red
    cabbage & lokse 65
  stuffed cabbage leaves 78
  stuffed roast duck with
    Moravian cabbage 62
cakes
  ducat cakes 107
  fruit cake 120
  mock saddle of venison cake
    119
  mole's cake 122
  pound cake 121
caraway
  baked trout with caraway 58
  garlic soup 28
carp 53, 55
  fried carp with potato salad
    56
carrots
  cold cod salad 43
  fresh carrot salad 19
cereals 18–19
cheese 20, 89
  fried bread with spicy
    stir-fry 49
  langos 100
  peach chicken & croquettes
    60
  potato pasta 86
  Slovak cheese pie 97
  Slovak pirohy 98
  spicy marinated cheese 40
  three fried dishes & chips 96
chicken 53, 55
  chicken noodle soup 30
  chicken pasta salad 44
  peach chicken & croquettes
    60
  red pepper chicken paprikas
    61
  Slovak schnitzel 67
chillies
  drowned sausages 45
  spicy marinated cheese 40
  stuffed peppers 69
chocolate
  mock saddle of venison cake
    119

cod
  cold cod salad 43
cream
  baked potatoes with cream 93
  kremes 115
  mole's cake 122
  potato pasta 86
  roast beef in creamy sauce
    76
  trout with cream sauce 59
  vegetarian potato goulash
    94
crêpes, sweet 112
crumpets 99
cucumber and tomato salad
  42
Czech Republic 6–7
  agriculture 11
  beer & winemaking 14–15
  festivals & traditions 16–17
  food culture & customs
    12–13
  geography 10–11
  history 8–9

D
dairy products 20
desserts 109, 111
dill
  beef with dill sauce 80
doughnuts with 'snow' 104
drowned sausages 45
ducat cakes 107
duck 55
  stuffed roast duck with
    Moravian cabbage 62
dumplings 13, 39, 59
  beef broth with dumplings
    31
  fruit dumplings 101
  lentil soup with dumplings 27
  pork & dumplings with
    horseradish sauce 71

E
eggs
  baked rice pudding 103
  'snow' 104
  Spanish birds 81

F
fish 21, 53, 55
flavourings 21
fresh carrot salad 19
fried bread with spicy stir-fry
  49

fried carp with potato salad 56
fruit 20
  baked rice pudding 103
  fruit cake 120
  fruit dumplings 101

G
game 21, 53, 55
garlic
  drowned sausages 45
  garlic soup 28
  meatloaf with tomato sauce
    75
goose 53, 55
  roast goose with red
    cabbage & lokse 65
goulash soup 32
grains 18–19

H
ham
  peach chicken & croquettes
    60
  vlassky salad snacks 46
herbs 21, 55
  spicy marinated cheese 40
honey
  sweet semolina pudding 102
hops 18
horseradish
  pork & dumplings with
    horseradish sauce 71

I
ingredients 18–19

K
ketchup 21
koblasa & thick pea sauce 72
kremes 115

L
lamb with creamy spinach 83
langos 100
lard 21, 55
lentil soup with dumplings 27
liver
  beef broth with dumplings
    31

M
meat 21, 53, 55
meatloaf with tomato sauce 75
mock saddle of venison cake
  119
mole's cake 122

mushrooms
   potato soup 29
   rabbit with mushroom sauce 85
mustard 21
   pork crackling pâté 48

N
noodles
   chicken noodle soup 30
nuts 19
   sweet semolina pudding 102

O
onions
   beef goulash 77
   cold cod salad 43
   cucumber & tomato salad 42
   drowned sausages 45
   meatloaf with tomato sauce 75
   pork crackling pâté 48
   Szegediner goulash 70

P
pasta
   chicken pasta salad 44
   pasta with poppy seeds 95
peach chicken & croquettes 60
peas
   koblasa & thick pea sauce 72
   vlassky salad snacks 46
peppers
   beef goulash 77
   chicken pasta salad 44
   red pepper chicken paprikas 61
   sweet pepper stew 92
plum jam 20
poppy seeds
   pasta with poppy seeds 95
   poppy seed roll 118
   potato skubanky 73
pork 53, 55
   fried bread with spicy stir-fry 49

meatloaf with tomato sauce 75
pork & dumplings with horseradish sauce 71
pork crackling pâté 48
potato dumplings with pork crackling 51
roast pork with sauerkraut 68
schnitzel 66
stuffed peppers 69
Szegediner goulash 70
potatoes
   baked potatoes with cream 93
   fried carp with potato salad 56
   goulash soup 32
   peach chicken & croquettes 60
   potato dumplings with pork crackling 51
   potato pancakes 41
   potato pasta 86
   potato skubanky 73
   potato soup 29
   roast goose with red cabbage & lokse 65
   Slovak schnitzel 67
   sour bean soup 26
   three fried dishes & chips 96
   vegetarian potato goulash 94
   vlassky salad snacks 46
poultry 21
pound cake 121
pulses 19

R
rabbit with mushroom sauce 85
raisins
   apple & cinnamon bread pudding 114
   apple strudel with raisins 113
red pepper chicken paprikas 61
rice
   baked rice pudding 103
   stuffed cabbage leaves 78
   stuffed peppers 69

roast beef in creamy sauce 76
roast goose with red cabbage & lokse 65
roast pork with sauerkraut 68
rye bread & rohlíky or rozky 124

S
saddle of venison 84
salads 39
sauces 21
sauerkraut 55
   roast pork with sauerkraut 68
   sauerkraut soup 34
   Szegediner goulash 70
sausages 39
   drowned sausages 45
   koblasa & thick pea sauce 72
   sour bean soup 26
schnitzel 66
semolina pudding, sweet 102
Slovak cheese pie 97
Slovak Easter bread 123
Slovak pirohy 98
Slovak schnitzel 67
Slovakia 6–7
   agriculture 11
   beer & winemaking 14–15
   food culture 12–13
   geography 11
   history 8–9
snacks 37, 39
soups 23, 25, 26–34
sour bean soup 26
Spanish birds 81
spices 21
   drowned sausages 45
   sauerkraut soup 34
   spicy marinated cheese 40
spinach
   lamb with creamy spinach 83
stuffed cabbage leaves 78
stuffed peppers 69
stuffed roast duck with Moravian cabbage 62
sweet buns 116
sweet crêpes 112

sweet main courses 89, 91
sweet pepper stew 92
sweet semolina pudding 102
Szegediner goulash 70

T
tartar sauce 96
three fried dishes & chips 96
tomatoes
   cucumber & tomato salad 42
   fried bread with spicy stir-fry 49
   meatloaf with tomato sauce 75
   sweet pepper stew 92
trout 53, 55
   baked trout with caraway 58
   trout with cream sauce 59

V
vanilla pudding 107
vegetables 19
   potato soup 29
   three fried dishes & chips 96
vegetarian dishes 87, 89
   vegetarian potato goulash 94
venison
   saddle of venison 84
vlassky salad snacks 46

W
walnuts
   mock saddle of venison cake 119
   walnut roll 118

Publisher's acknowledgements
The publishers would like to thank the following for permission to reproduce their images:
Alamy p6t Lebrecht Music and Arts Photo Library; p6bl INTERFOTO; p6br Isifa Image Service s.r.o.; p7t Stefan Sollfors; p7b Peter Horree; p8t The Art Gallery Collection; p8b INTERFOTO;

p9tl Lebrecht Music and Arts Photo Library; p9tr Imagestate Media Partners Ltd – Impact Photos; p10t JTB Photo Communications, Inc.; p10b Ball Miwako; p12bl Greg Balfour Evans; p12m Picture Contact BV; p12r Travelstock44; p13t Viktor Fischer; p14t Alberto Paredes; p14b Lonely Planet Images; p15tl Vladimir Cuvala; p15tr

Imagebroker; p15b Peter Forsberg; p16l Ragnarok; p16m Lonely Planet Images; p16br Brenda Kean; p17 INTERFOTO; p18bl Nick Dunmur.
t=top, b=bottom, r=right, l=left, m=middle.
All other photographs © Anness Publishing Ltd.